How to Grow Your Business Using Social Media

&

YouTube Channel Success

By

Ernie Braveboy

Get Your Free Copy of

How to be a Real Estate Millionaire

To Get Your Free Copy, Open the Link

https://ebraveboy_3ee2.gr8.com/

TABLE OF CONTENTS

HOW TO GROW YOUR BUSINESS USING SOCIAL MEDIA..7

Introduction 9

Why Should You Care About Building A Strong Social Media Presence? 11

Growing Your Business Using Facebook 17

Growing Your Business Using Instagram.........................26

Growing Your Business Using YouTube..........................33

Growing Your Business Using Twitter.............................41

Growing Your Business Using LinkedIn..........................47

Growing Your Business Using Snapchat..........................55

Growing Your Business Using Pinterest..........................61

Conclusion..69

YOUTUBE CHANNEL SUCCESS 71

Introduction 73

Section 1: Laying The Foundation..................................75

Getting Started with YouTube: Why YouTube?................75

The Riches Are In The Niches: Why And How To Choose A Niche For Your YouTube Channel 79

Setting Up: Creating Your YouTube Channel Fast 87

Your Essential YouTube Creator Equipment Guide 90

Section 2: Growing Your Channel - How To Create A Great YouTube Channel & Gain Millions Of Subscribers 94

How to Create a Great YouTube Channel that Has a Rabid Following and Million of Subscribers 94

Youtube Growth Hacking: Optimizing YouTube Content For Search And Improved Views And Subscribers 100

YouTube SEO Hacks: The Important Elements To Optimize...... 104

Section 3: YouTube Monetization - How To Implement The Most Effective YouTube Monetization Strategies 114

YouTube Monetization Strategies: How To Monetize Your YouTube Channel For Recurring Passive Income 115

Conclusion 123

How to Grow Your Business Using Social Media

Create an Awesome Online Presence on Facebook, Instagram, YouTube, LinkedIn, Snapchat, And Many More

By

Ernie Braveboy

INTRODUCTION

I want to thank you and congratulate you for buying the book, "How To Grow Your Business Using Social Media: Create An Awesome Online Presence On Facebook, Instagram, YouTube, LinkedIn, Snapchat, And Many More."

Are you looking for a strong online presence? Are you looking to generate more traffic that converts? Are you looking to expand your customer or client base? Do you want to generate strong leads? Do you want to sell more products?

Whatever your business interest is, leveraging the power of social media is something you cannot sweep under the rug. Today, the power of social media is stronger than ever before. People are starting small businesses from scratch and building them into huge successful brands just by using social media. Orabrush and SEOmoz are examples of companies that have become enormously successful by following this path.

We are also seeing a rising number of people becoming famous and establishing huge followings on social media. PewDiePie is one such example. He began creating videos on Youtube about video games and today he has a whooping following of approximately 66 million subscribers, with a total net worth of approximately $20 million! There are many other inspiring stories like his like Justin Bieber.

Even the major household names are jumping onto the bandwagon and are aggressively using the power of social media to become even more successful. Pampers, Nike, and Domino's are examples that can testify to this. The number of success stories thanks to social media is phenomenal. The bottom-line, it is big and it is continuously growing.

As a business owner, you do not want to be left behind on this. There has never been a better time of using the power of social media to grow your business than now. By choosing to incorporate social media as part of your main business strategy, you stand a higher chance of doing far better than you are right now.

The challenge is that with all this popularity of social media, there still remains one challenge; if you do not do it the right way, you do not stand a chance. But lucky for you, if you have no clue about how or where to start, do not panic. This book will be your friend. The main purpose of this book is to provide you with the right guidance to navigate the competitive world of social media successfully. You will learn how to harness the power of the main social media platforms out there to build your brand and grow your business.

By the time you are done reading the material in this book, you will be way ahead of the pack because you will have gained a competitive edge that allows you to thwart the efforts of your competitors.

Are you ready? Let's get started.

Thanks again for buying this book. I hope you enjoy it!

Before we can start discussing how to use different social media platforms to grow your business, it is important that we start by understanding why you need to prioritize social media marketing and why now is the best time to get in.

WHY SHOULD YOU CARE ABOUT BUILDING A STRONG SOCIAL MEDIA PRESENCE?

Knowing why something is important is a key motivator. You will be putting a lot of time, effort and even money in this so it makes a lot of sense if you know what you stand to gain by doing it. So what can you expect from investing your time, energy and money into social media marketing?

Here are some of these ways:

1.   You increase brand awareness

As a business owner, few things are more important than visibility. Can you imagine running a business that no one knows about? Think about it this way; imagine that you have established a small shop for selling confectionaries. You then decide to secretly run the shop within your own compound without anyone knowing. What are the chances of that business succeeding? The chances are exactly zero.

As a person who owns a business, getting the word out to as many people as you can is vital to the success of your brand. Social media is a very effective tool for doing just that. Social media takes the process of creating brand awareness to a whole new level.

Take Facebook for instance. Facebook happens to be one of the most powerful social media platforms in the world today and is incredibly useful for creating brand awareness. You can create a page for your business on Facebook and start sharing posts with information about your business or whatever you are selling to your friends. If your friends find the posts you share appealing, they can share with their own friends who may then spread the word out further, thereby creating a multiplier effect.

In case you are wondering, this is how viral marketing works. By investing a little effort on social media, you have the power of marketing your brand to a huge number of people in a more efficient way.

2. You can interact with your target audience

Huge successful brands know how important building a relationship of trust is to the success of their businesses. That is why they invest billions of dollars in Customer Relationship Management (CRM) software solutions and customer support portals. This helps them keep in touch and be more available to their customers on demand.

However, you do not need to invest in such expensive infrastructure, especially if you are a small business. That would be counterproductive. A smarter way of going about it would be using social media. Social media provides a great way to establish a communication channel between you and your audience that is two-way.

By doing this, they will be able to interact with you, providing useful feedback and asking questions about your product. This is the foundation of building trust with your customers so that they will be more open to doing business with you again. You will also get a chance to improve your products or services and marketing strategies in a way that suits your audience. You can get all this at an almost if not free cost. Just imagine that.

3. Social media is cost-effective

One of the main things that challenge business owners from time to time is the cost of doing business. For instance, the cost of promoting your business to create brand awareness through traditional channels of advertising e.g. TV, radio and newspapers can easily drive costs through the roof. If you are someone who is just starting out, this can greatly discourage you. Many times, this game is often left to the big players with deep pockets.

But with the proliferation of social media today, the tables have turned. Today, you do not need a lot of money to promote your business on social media. In fact, you may not need any money at all. Sure, there are times when you may find it convenient to pay for some services, but even that comes at a cost that many can easily afford.

4. Increases traffic and conversions

Increasing traffic and ultimately conversions is the main goal of anyone who relies on the internet to do business. This is how you end up getting more customers, clients or make more sales. However, you need an effective strategy to make people come to your site (aka driving traffic), otherwise, you may as well pack up and go home.

You may have heard of the popular dogma, "Build and they will come." In the early days of the internet, this was very true. Very few people had ventured online so anyone who had the balls of setting up a website would have a stream of visitors in no time. This is how companies like Google and Yahoo managed to thrive into the successful companies they are today.

However, today the strategy of, "Build and they will come" never works. You may end up wasting your time and money if you do it this way. As of this writing, there are an estimated 440 million blogs on the internet. And that is just in blogging. There is so much competition that nobody could care less about your website if you made no effort of trying to get their attention.

This is where social media comes in. There are such a huge number of people hanging out on social media that you can easily turn it into your main source of traffic. The efforts of advertising on social media are likely to perform far better than relying on traditional methods of advertising.

5.   Improved loyalty

Anyone who has experienced the life of an entrepreneur understands the importance of customer loyalty. Loyal customers in your business will make more repeated purchases and over time, your business will stabilize and grow. Loyal customers are the greatest asset of any business, and that includes yours.

Social media provides an unmatched way of creating a bond with your customers that will create loyalty. As previously stated, social media provides a two-way system of engaging with your customers. This enables you to connect with your customers on a more personal level.

You get valuable feedback, answer questions about your product, and provide customer support. When your prospects feel like that are valued and cared for, they will tend to develop trust with your brand. Therefore, you have a high chance of retaining them for the long term.

6. You get to keep track of your competitors

No matter what kind of business you are running or whatever industry you are operating in, there is always competition. Dealing with competition is always part of life in business.

You need to always be aware of what your competition is doing or the changes that are happening in your industry; otherwise, you are likely to fall behind drastically in your business. Fortunately, for you, social media comes in handy when it comes to this.

Since social media became prevalent in the world of business, it has completely revolutionized the way you can keep tabs on your competition. Social media has made it amazingly simple for you to see what your competitor is doing, and either learn from what is working best or come up with effective countermeasures.

By simply following them and going through the comments of their customers, you are able to gain valuable insights into how you can better deal with competition.

All things considered, social media is a very beneficial tool for carrying out business. The benefits we have discussed in this chapter are just a tip of the iceberg. If you become more open to implementing social media in your way of doing business, you will realize that it offers more benefits than you could ever imagine.

Now that you are aware of the main benefits of using social media, let's begin by looking at how you can start using the most powerful social media platform right now, Facebook.

GROWING YOUR BUSINESS USING FACEBOOK

Earlier, I described Facebook as the most popular and powerful social media platform- it may have powerful rivals like Twitter and Instagram, but it still holds its position as the most powerful and popular.

As of 2018, Alexa ranks Facebook as the third most visited website on the planet. Statista, on the other hand, reports that Facebook has approximately 2.23 billion active monthly users as of the 2nd quarter of 2018. This not only supports the argument that it is the most powerful social media giant, but also one of the most popular websites in the world.

With all this popularity and wide user base, Facebook has become the ultimate business tool in the online world. This explains why most people and companies in the business view it as the go-to place for their marketing needs

The goal of this chapter is to show you how you can start effectively using Facebook as a tool to grow your business today. There are several ways of using Facebook to grow your business. However, they don't all work the same. Some ways deliver very insignificant results that are not even worth your time.

It is for this reason that I have chosen to show you the best and most powerful ways you can use Facebook to power your business. You can make a personal choice on what techniques you prefer but I recommend that you practice all the strategies covered here. Over time, you will be in a better position to stick with the methods that work best for you.

Let's begin.

Method 1: Create a Facebook page

A business page is one of the most powerful tools that Facebook provides. It offers various features that are vital to a business. For instance, a Facebook page has a call to action, a Messenger chat widget, and an appointment scheduling form. These features come in handy when you want to establish relationships with your customers or prospects.

In addition, a Facebook page provides a way to provide your contact information, give information about the products or services that you offer, and other vital information. It also allows your customers to provide a rating for your business and provide honest reviews about the products and services you offer.

And the good thing is that a Facebook page is the fastest way you can create an online presence for your business on Facebook. It acts like a personal Facebook profile, only that the name on the profile is your business.

If you want to create a Facebook page, first log in to your Facebook account. If you do not have one, create it at www.facebook.com. Then, click on the link on the top right corner that is labeled "Create". A drop-down menu will appear. Click on "page". Then follow the steps in the process and you will have a Facebook page created in a matter of minutes.

After creating a page, the next challenge you have is to get a huge number of likes, engage your followers and keep the number growing. You can begin by inviting your friends on Facebook to like the page. You can also ask them to invite their Facebook friends too. This is a simple but effective way to grow your page likes. We will discuss how you can automate the process later when we cover Facebook ads.

So how exactly can a Facebook page help you to grow your business? Here is how:

- You can create posts and share them on the page so that your page fans can see them.

- You can create advertisements that can be viewed by any number of people, depending on your audience. We will cover Facebook ads later on. For now, you just need to know that you will need a Facebook page to create them.

- You can communicate with your customers through the Messenger widget and inbox

- Your customers can comment on your posts or advertisements, providing valuable feedback on your product or service.

Method 2: Create A Facebook Group

The next best powerful tool to use to grow your business on Facebook in groups.

So what is a Facebook group?

A Facebook group is simply a virtual way of bringing together persons with common interests, of the same community, who belong to the same club or who belong to a 'cult'.

This is done so that they can have a way of talking to each other and share ideas more effectively. The thing with Facebook groups is that Facebook allows conversations within groups to appear within the

Timelines of the members, which means you can easily reach and engage more people with a Facebook group, without even spending any money.

A Facebook group works best if you want to offer customized yet group support for your products/services. This is because, within the group, the members can as well help one another, depending on what they have learned while interacting with you and much more

Creating a Facebook group is a rather simple task too. Simply click on the Create link on the top right corner of your Facebook home page and click Group on the drop-down menu that appears. On the pop-up that appears, give your group a name; add a number of friends as members, mark it as either private or open and click create. That is all there is to it.

A group can be used to promote your business in the following ways:

- You can invite your friends to join the group. You can also send out emails to potential customers asking them to join the group. The key here is to organize a group of people who may have interests in the product or service you are offering so that they can communicate freely and share ideas.

- Create discussions around recent developments in your industry. If you can get people talking about things happening in your industry, they'll likely buy from you in the future.

- Announce to the group periodically about the products and services that you offer.

- You can create and promote events in the group. Those who attend the events will get a chance to buy products and services from you, perhaps at a discount for instance.

The purpose of creating a group is to bring together your best fans and create a community. The more people you can add to this community, the better. Your focus should be on engaging this community as much as possible. A highly engaged community of loyal followers can end up creating customers who buy from you regularly. Also, the more active your group becomes, the higher the chances of Facebook recommending your group by showing it on the sidebar. This can make your book even more popular.

Method 3: Create a Facebook Ad

Another powerful tool available to you as is Facebook Ads. In the history of advertising, there has never been an advertising platform that offers so much flexibility. With Facebook ads, you are able to deliver your targeted message through ads to a specific audience of your own choosing. This means that you are able to sell to the people who are more likely to buy from you. As a result, your ads stand a chance of converting better.

In traditional advertising such as radio and TV, your marketing efforts are likely to go to waste because you don't end up capturing the attention of the right people. Facebook gives the option of tweaking various parameters so that your advertisements end up being served to the right people, which means that the conversion rates are a lot higher.

The process of creating a Facebook Ad is simple but detailed. It is so detailed that it could easily take up a book of its own. However, there is no shortage of helpful guides out there to help you out. Furthermore, Facebook has gone to great lengths to make the process of creating an Ad dummy simple and self-explanatory. I would recommend that you read guides from Hubspot and Adespresso. They cover every detail about the process in the best way possible.

You can use Facebook Ads to grow your business in a number of ways some of which I will list below:

- You can carry out ad campaigns to increase the number of likes on your Facebook page. This can increase the number of customers you will have in the long term.

- You can conduct ad campaigns to increase traffic to your website. If you run an online business, this can directly help you sell more products or services and boost your revenue.

- You can conduct ad campaigns to increase awareness about your brand and product offerings.

- You can increase the reach of your Facebook posts. If you do not have a massive following on your Facebook page in the beginning, it can get really difficult to get a huge number of people to view it. However, Facebook offers you an option of boosting the reach by paying a small advertising fee and you get a huge number of people to view it.

- You can create promotional video posts and have them viewed by a huge number of people by running a video ad campaign. We will talk about video ads in the next section.

Method 4: Create a Facebook Video Ad

The next best tool that is at your disposal as a business owner is Facebook Video Ads. Up until recently, people have relied on text and image ads. However, top internet marketers are now waking up to the fact that video ads are performing by far better than any other type of ad format. In fact, research by Socialbakers reveals that Facebook videos get more reach than any other type of content.

This is because Facebook users enjoy content that is very engaging. Videos are especially known to be very engaging on Facebook and in all the other social media sites. This essentially means leveraging the power of video ads can bring surprising results than you may ever imagine.

So how do you create video ads on Facebook?

It's actually quite simple. If you have created an Ad as we discussed previously, then you are pretty familiar with the process. You just need to follow the same process but change your ad objective to "Get video views." In case you get stuck, just read this tutorial created by Wordstream.

If you do not know how to create videos, do not panic, there exist many service providers today that can help you with the process of creating video ads. They make the process of creating videos so simple that anyone could simply do it. I recommend Biteable.com and Shakr.com. You will, however, need to pay a small fee after creating your video just to remove the watermarks. You could also hire someone through Fiverr.com- services here begin at $5!

If you want your video ad campaigns to convert better, follow these guidelines:

- Make sure your video is as short as possible. Users on social media are mostly skimmers and as such, they are easily distracted. If your video is too long, they may just skip it and move on. A general rule is to make your videos no more than 20 seconds long.

- Create a video thumbnail that sparks interest and curiosity for the Facebook user.

- Optimize for mobile devices if the user is connected to Wi-Fi. This is in part because mobile users switch off the auto-play option so that they can save on their data plans. Also, if they have a poor connection, your video may stop playing and you may end up paying for videos that are not likely to convert.

- Ensure you announce your main message early on in the video. As I said previously, Facebook users have little patience. They may decide within the first few seconds that they need to move on to another post. If you pack your main message late in the video, chances are that few people will get it.

- Create videos that don't require sound. People browse their newsfeeds mostly to kill time. In most cases, they are not interested in listening to the message in the video. You could try adding captions to the video in case you are worried that your message may not be clear.

As you can note from the discussion, Facebook is an indispensable tool you should not ignore if you are serious about creating an online presence and growing your business online. The marketing strategies discussed in this chapter are highly powerful and many successful businesses use them every single day so do your best to master them. You may even find yourself becoming an expert at marketing businesses as you try out the strategies covered here, making you the go-to guy of Facebook marketing within your circle of influence.

Obviously, as you well know, 'the devil lies in the details'. You will not just create a Facebook page, group or ad and expect to become an instant hit. What matters is for you to be consistent in everything you do if you really want to stand out and build a following that is eagerly waiting to hear from you. As a rule, don't always just post 'buy my product' messages as your status updates. You could post 'behind the scenes content', inspiring messages, ask questions that get people to give their opinions, post contests and much more to keep your readers engaged.

GROWING YOUR BUSINESS USING INSTAGRAM

Instagram is another social media platform that is enjoying massive popularity. It started in 2010 as a simple photo sharing application on iOS. As time went by, it added photo filters to polish the look and feel of images as well as social media features like profiles, followers and comments. And in 2012, it launched the app for the Android platform, which made it so popular that Facebook bought it for 1 billion dollars.

As of June 2018, Instagram is reported to have an excess of 1 billion active users. This wide user base makes it even more popular than Twitter, which has an active user base of 336 million. This wide popularity has generated a lot of interest from marketers and business people alike.

This chapter will teach you how you can use Instagram to grow your business.

Instagram Strategies To Grow Your Business

Strategy 1: Polishing up your Instagram profile

The first strategy is the simplest, but one which you can easily get wrong if you are sloppy. It helps to get started on the right foot before you can get to the more advanced stuff.

This step involves setting up an appropriate business account on Instagram, the way the big brands do. Since setting up an account is a pretty straightforward process; I will only highlight the main areas that you need to pay close attention.

HOW TO GROW YOUR BUSINESS USING SOCIAL MEDIA

1. Firstly, make sure that your profile photo is impactful. To avoid any confusion, it is best that you only include your business logo. This way, many people will be able to identify your brand very quickly.

2. Next, you will need to write up your account name appropriately. As for this, just include the name of your business and you will be good to go. Also, remember not to sign up with your Facebook account. Create a separate business email account and use it. Your Instagram business account and personal Facebook account should be separate.

3. After that, you will have to include the name of your company in the username too.

4. Then, write up a great bio; this is one place that you may need to take some time. In this part, you are communicating whatever your business offers. You only have a 150-word restriction, so brevity is vital. In a specific language that is clear, explain your proposition, the products or services that you offer as well as a way that potential customers can find you. For an idea of how a great Instagram bio should look like, check out this post by Later.com.

5. Adding a link to your website is also a good idea. This is also done in the bio section. Make sure you add the URL of your website too. You have the liberty to change this information as many times as you wish.

Now you have a professional looking business profile that is optimized for getting the most value possible.

Strategy 2: Promote Your Business Using Instagram Photos

The next method that is incredibly powerful at promoting your business is regularly posting content, in this case, photos. This is especially true if you own a business that sells products.

You may have heard the popular cliché, "A picture is worth a thousand words." This rule applies to social media marketing, especially when it comes to Instagram. The very success of the platform itself is thanks to the way it tends to be image-centered. The users of the platform respond very well to strikingly beautiful images. You can make this feature an important aspect of your marketing strategy and stand to see some great results.

The way to do this is to take some really great product photos and simply post them on the app. Now, this doesn't mean that you take just any blurry and crappy looking photo and post it and hope for great results to come your way. No, it simply won't happen. You have to do better. Many great photos are posted on the site every day. If yours do not warrant any attention, you won't get any. You have to put in the effort to make them look good.

Follow the guidelines below in case you are clueless:

1. Make sure all your images have a professional look and feel. Make sure the lighting is good. Save your images at double the resolution size so that you can preserve the image quality.

2. Make sure your images are square in shape. Instagram automatically crops images to the size of 612 by 612 pixels. If your images are not square, you will lose entire sections of the image. Use Photoshop to adjust image size to 1024 by

1024 pixels. That way, they will maintain their quality even after processing.

3. Use Instagram's filters to edit the look and feel of the images.

Strategy 3: Promote Your Business Using Instagram Videos

Another type of content that creates a lot of engagement on Instagram is videos. In the previous chapter, we talked about the power of video posts on Facebook. Apparently, videos tend to have the same effect on every social media platform, not just Facebook. If a fad is anything to go by, I would say that video marketing is the latest fad in online marketing.

That is why I am going to recommend it even on Instagram. Instagram allows you to post videos of up to 60 seconds on the platform. It also offers a number of filters that you can apply to every video post. There is a number of ways you can use this opportunity to grow your business and enhance its popularity. They include:

1. You can create a behind the scenes type of video about your business. This means that you can shoot something along the lines of how you create your products, how a typical day at the place of business looks, how the backstage looked during an event you organized and anything creative that comes to mind. This creates transparency and your customers will feel more connected to your business.

2. You could create a bunch of how-to videos. How-to content is the hallmark of content creation and is the most sought-after type of content. If you create one video, which for instance, shows how

your product can be used to solve a certain problem, you can bet that a lot of people will watch it and the impact it will have on your business will be positive.

3. Create a video showcasing the products or services that you offer. Remember not to focus on your product only. That makes you sound boring and spammy. Try to emulate TV commercials. Create an entertaining video and make your product a part of the video.

4. Post-user-generated content. This is content that has been created by fans and users of your product. It not only gives you less work to do but also creates a bond of trust between your business and the public.

Let's now move to the next strategy, which is Instagram Ads.

Strategy 4: Promote Your Business Using Instagram Ads

Instagram Ads is yet another powerful tool that you can use to promote your business and grow it. Instagram ads are a good option especially if you run a business that focuses on visuals such as, restaurants, fashion, art, jewelry, auto-motives and the like.

One of the advantages of Instagram ads is that they are integrated and implemented by Facebook's ad placement system. As such, you get the same level of granular control that you get with Facebook ads.

With Instagram, you get the option of creating 5 types of ads. You have the option of creating a **photo ad, a video ad, a slideshow and, a story ad** or **carousel ad**. Photo ads and video ads are something you are already familiar with. They are just sponsored versions of photo and video posts. Slideshow ads are quite similar to video ads only that they are made up of still images with cool transitions and perhaps a bit of text and audio.

A carousel ad is made up of a collection of photos or videos. They are especially good if you want to showcase a wide variety of products. A story ad, on the other hand, is a new and special type of ad. It exists at the top section of the news feed (the story section). The story section is made up of a set of continuous content, which is displayed in full screen, much like what you see in Whatsapp status updates. Story ads blend in with the stories. They are a good way of creating brand awareness.

The process of creating an Instagram ad is pretty much the same as creating a Facebook ad. In fact, all Instagram ads are created in Facebook's Ad Manager. You just have to link your Facebook page with your Instagram accounts and follow the same process. The only difference is the ad placement section. You have to explicitly declare that you want your ad to appear on Instagram only. Read this post by Shopify for complete instructions on how to create Instagram ads.

To summarize, the power of Instagram is not to be underestimated. It has the backing of the biggest social media giant and with that comes many advantages. By choosing to ride along, you will be secretly giving yourself a competitive edge. This chapter has shown you the easiest ways to get started. Now, the ball is in your court. If you implement the advice provided in this chapter, you will be surprised how fast things will change for you.

Up next, we will be looking at how YouTube can be used to power your business.

GROWING YOUR BUSINESS USING YOUTUBE

Another popular platform that you can use to enhance your presence online and even get more customers is YouTube. If used well, this platform can work wonders for you.

Currently, YouTube is ranked by Bustle as the second most popular website in the world. Over 1.8 billion people visit the site each month. This has led to this website being referred to as the second most popular search engine in the world with over 300 hours of content being uploaded every minute, 4.5 billion videos being watched every single day and over 30 million visitors daily! With these stats, you cannot help but want to be part of the content creators.

Apart from being a huge warehouse for hosting video content, the platform incorporates social media features such as user profiles, channels, commenting, likes, subscriptions, video sharing, and live videos.

Countless businesses and people have used the platform and its features to market themselves with outstanding success. This chapter will show you how you can leverage the amazing power of this platform to grow your business and make it popular. Let's begin.

YouTube Strategies To Grow Your Business

Strategy 1: Create a YouTube Channel

There is always the first step with anything and in our case i.e. using YouTube for business, the first step is to create a channel. Like most things on the internet, creating a YouTube channel is a rather trivial task.

First, you have to sign in with your Google account and then click the settings icon in the top right corner. You will see the link "Create a channel." Click on it and follow the steps in the process and you will have created a channel in a matter of minutes.

That's just the basics though- you need to do more than just create a channel. There are a few things to keep in mind when creating a YouTube channel for your business. They are:

- Create great channel art and include your logo in the channel art. A channel art is like the cover photo on your Facebook Page. For ideas on how to create a great cover art, you can check out the YouTube channels of other great brands and find some inspiration.

- Write up a good description. Like on Instagram, you will need to take your time here. What you write here really counts since it will be crawled by search engines and shows up in channel suggestions by YouTube. Read this amazing tutorial by Biteable.com on how to create an amazing description.

- Add links to your cover art. YouTube offers you options to add links to your YouTube channel art. This could mean including links to your other social media accounts and your website.

- Create a great channel trailer. This is the video that visitors first see the moment they visit your channel. A short, attention-grabbing and informative video would work well here. Once again, sample other successful YouTube channels to learn what works.

- Include your contact information in the "About" section of your channel.

Now you have a great YouTube channel that matches up the quality of your competitors. So, what next?

Strategy 2: Create And Post Video Content.

You may have heard the phrase, "content is king." Well, that applies to many places and YouTube happens to be one of those places. If you want to get a chance of making your brand and channel popular, you have to post a lot of videos on your YouTube channel regularly. YouTube users are always hungry for new content. If you are up to the task, they will reward you with loyalty.

You can take different approaches to create content for your channel for purposes of promoting your band. Some of them include the following:

1. You can interview the staff, owners, shareholders, customers, partners, or even have someone interview you.

2. You can create short how-to tutorials on how people can use the product your business offers.

3. You can create a small documentary on the history of your company or business or simply a company profile.

4. You can create small, TV-style advertisements for your products.

In general, anything you come up with is fine as long as it is not boring and mundane. Videos that tend to do well come up as mysterious, engaging, interesting and useful. If you create something along those lines, you will never go wrong.

Strategy 3: Promote Your Videos And Channel For More Subscribers

The next thing you need to do is to promote your channel and content. Your channel may not do as well as you may think if you do not find a way to promote it. Sure, there is a lot of organic traffic from YouTube itself, but when you are just starting out, you will need to put in the work before you ever get noticed and recommended by YouTube.

Let's discuss how to go about it:

1. You can share your videos on other social media platforms such as Facebook, Twitter, Instagram and the like. Encourage your friends to share the video as much as they can. Over time, as your views increase in number, you will start getting noticed.

2. If you have a blog or website, you can embed the videos in your posts or even offer them to the subscribers in your mailing lists. This can also be a great source of traffic.

3. Ensure that you craft great titles for your YouTube videos and make sure to include keywords. Including keywords will increase the chances of your videos showing up whenever people search for those terms on YouTube or Google. Crafting great YouTube titles is an art by itself. For useful tips on how to do it, you can read these posts by SearchEngineLand and Wirebuzz.

4. Include a call to action in your videos. Do not let any viewer of your video go scot-free. Encourage them to like and subscribe to your channel at the end of your videos. Surprisingly, many will respond if they liked the video you posted. Before you know it, you will have turned many viewers into subscribers.

5. Make sure your video thumbnails are eye-catching or intriguing. If you spend a lot of time on YouTube, you may have noticed that you tend to click on videos whose thumbnails pique your interest and have an interesting title. Such is the power of combining great title with thumbnails.

6. Lastly, you can create ads to boost your viewership. Read on to find out more about YouTube Ads

Strategy 4: Creating YouTube Ads

Almost every social media platform out there has an advertising option and YouTube is no exception. Your business can benefit greatly by tapping into this power to get the word out about what you do or sell.

YouTube Ads are powered by Google AdWords. Therefore, if you want to create ads for the YouTube platform, you have to sign up for an Adwords account. YouTube offers six types of ads. They are:

1. **Skippable ads:** These are also known as TrueView ads. These are ads that play for up to five seconds before they give viewers an option of skipping. These are considered to be the best ads to engage potential customers. You only pay for these ads if the video plays for more than 30 seconds. This makes them a safer investment because you only get to pay for viewers that are genuinely interested in viewing your ad and are likely to convert.

2. **Non-skippable ads:** This type of ad plays to the end and cannot be skipped. You pay for this type of ad on a CPM basis. CPM means cost per one thousand impressions. As you can guess, this type of ad can get annoying to many viewers. Therefore, they are made to be typically shorter than 15 seconds long to make them tolerable.

3. **Bumper ads:** This type of ad is similar to the non-skippable ad. The only difference is that it tends to be very short. It typically lasts for six seconds. You also pay for it on a CPM basis.

4. **Overlay ads:** These simple banner ads appear at the bottom of a video and fade out afterward. They can either be image-based or text-based.

5. **Display ads:** These ads may also appear at the top of the right column that is reserved for suggested videos.

6. **Cards and sponsored ads:** Lastly, these type of ads essentially call to action pop-ups that appear within the player. They are less annoying because they only expand to full size when the viewer clicks on them.

Creating an Ad for YouTube is a pretty straightforward process too. You first need to link your YouTube account to Adwords. Simply log in to your AdWords dashboard, click "Linked YouTube accounts", and follow the steps from there.

There are many helpful resources online to guide you throughout the process of creating your first campaign, in case you feel intimidated. I personally find these guides from Hubspot and Searchenginewatch to be especially helpful.

There are a few tips you need to keep in mind if you want to get the most out of YouTube ads. They include:

- Make your videos as short as possible. Usually, people will want to skip your ad as soon as they can. It gets even worse if they find it long and boring.

- Communicate your main message as early as possible. If you get your message across within the first five seconds, you will get the chance to communicate to as many people as you can, even if they end up skipping the video. This can work in your favor especially if brand awareness was your goal.

- Make sure you select the most appropriate ad type. There is no one-size-fits-all ad type. This will depend on your situation. For instance, skippable ads are better if you want to create brand awareness. Display ads can work well if you are selling products online.

- Lastly, make sure you research your audience well and target them through the targeting options provided. The more targeted your ad is, the more likely it is that they will convert.

YouTube is a viable option for building an online presence and even creating a loyal following. This is especially true if you consider the engaging nature of videos in social media platforms today. YouTube helps you take advantage of that in a platform that is already powered by videos themselves.

Hopefully, this chapter has pointed you in the direction. As you continue to implement the advice you have gotten, you will begin discovering other techniques that work better for your type of business and stick with them for their long-term benefit.☐

In the next chapter, we will cover the use of Twitter in growing your business.

GROWING YOUR BUSINESS USING TWITTER

Another great option you can explore in your quest for growing your business and enhancing its online image is to use Twitter. Jack Dorsey, Noah Glass, Biz Stone, and Evan Williams launched Twitter in 2006. The website allows sharing short messages called tweets with people who follow you. A tweet is a message that is made up of up to 280 characters. You can also include web links as well as pictures or videos in your tweets.

As of 2018, Twitter has a user base of approximately, 336 million, according to reports by Statista. With a user base like that, it is not difficult to see that the platform has massive potential for growing your business.

This chapter will show you how you can use Twitter to accomplish your growth endeavors and build up a huge loyal following.

Strategies You Can Use To Grow Your Business With Twitter

Strategy 1: Build A Great Profile

Your Twitter account and profile are the foundation on which everything else is built. Therefore, doing it right is a matter of utmost importance. If you have a complete and strategically constructed profile, you can create an element of trust with your potential customers and fans. It also improves how you appear in search results.

Creating a Twitter account is a straightforward process, so I am not going to go into details of how you can create one-all you need is to go to Twitter.com and follow the prompts. You should, however, do the following in order to have a great profile:

1. Make sure that your username or handle contains the name of your business. People will be using it to find your business, so you should make sure you name it appropriately. Avoid punctuation marks so that it becomes easier for people using mobile phones to type it. In case your name has been taken, you can create one that is similar.

2. Next, the profile photo should contain the logo of your brand. The profile header, which is positioned behind the profile picture should also be able to tell something about your business. You can include anything like say, showcase a promotion that you have, an upcoming event, or some news concerning your business.

3. Make sure that you craft a great bio. A great bio can go a long way in marketing your business, so time spent crafting a good bio is time well spent. You only have a word-limit of 280 words so you need to make every word count. For great ideas on how to create a bio that acts as bait for followers, read his post by Postplanner.

4. Lastly, make sure that your profile gets verified. A verified checkmark on your profile communicates authenticity. People will trust you and your content more, once your account gets verified. Steps on how to get verified can be found here.

Strategy 2: Start Following People

When you start out, you will not immediately get a huge number of followers. You have to start small. You do this by following people first. As you follow people, you will start finding that they follow you back. You can as well unfollow those who do not follow you back. The number of your followers will start increasing and you can start working your way up.

In general, you should follow people who fall under these categories:

- People who have been your customers before

- Your business partners, suppliers, and contractors

- Your competitors

- Trade organizations and professional bodies within your industry

- Businesses that are located within your neighborhood

- Businesses owned by people within your circle of influence.

Once you establish a small following, you can start creating content that engages your followers.

Strategy 3: Share Engaging Content

I have said this before and it is still worth repeating. In most cases, content really is king. When you share content that is engaging and useful to your audience, they can't help but be moved by it. So this should be a key part of your strategy in business, providing value.

If for instance, you run a blog, you can research and create useful how-to content that helps a reader solve a pressing problem. You can even write about how a product or service that you sell can help solve a problem. As I said before, how-to content is sought after by many people.

You can bet that your followers will appreciate and love content like this. Chances are very high that if they like it, they will retweet it, and up goes your number of followers.

Strategy 4: Create More Engagement With Multimedia Content

Even though text content can create a decent amount of engagement, nothing creates more engagement in social media platforms than multimedia content. You can engage your fans and even get more followers by doing the following

1. Sharing photos

Marketing research depicts that tweets that have photos are retweeted more than tweets that are just plainly text-based. Therefore, if you want to engage your followers more and have them massively promote your shared content, adding images can do the trick.

Simply adding appealing images to most of your tweets is all it takes. On top of that, you can communicate offers in these images. For instance, you could communicate the discounts that you are offering or even a contest that you have launched.

2. Sharing videos

The reason for doing this should be clear to you by now. Nothing engages users more than video; the power of videos on social media now is phenomenal. It is reported that the majority of Twitter users (around 79%) would rather watch video content than spend time reading the text. Further revelations in the report have shown that up to 84% of users who watched videos were inspired to make a purchase.

This should tell you that if you are not using video in your Twitter promotions, then you are missing on a lot of great opportunity to grow your business. You can create product tutorials, entertainment content or even tell a story. Whatever you do, just remember that posting videos is a smart strategy.

3. Sharing Gifs

Have you seen one of those animated pictures that seem to be moving but seem to be stuck in an infinite loop? Those are gifs. Gifs are another powerful way of creating engagement on Twitter. They are typically cheeky, funny and some arouse a lot of curiosity. Because of that, they tend to generate a lot of retweets and more following. They can also be a powerful way of promoting your business on Twitter.

You can read this post to learn how to create great promotional gifs for your business.

Strategy 5: Use Twitter Advertising

As I said before, nearly every platform comes with advertising options today and Twitter is no different- it is how these platforms generate revenue anyway! Advertisements are a great way of getting things done faster. By offering to pay for ads, you can do many things that would take the average person a lot of time and effort to accomplish.

With regards to paid promotions, Twitter offers three types of ad. These are **promoted accounts, promoted tweets** and **promoted trends**. Promoted accounts work by providing your selected audience with suggested accounts to follow. They are good for creating brand awareness and for getting more followers.

Promoted tweets, on the other hand, are meant to give more exposure to the content that you will be sharing on the platform. They are especially good if you are trying to communicate offers, create brand awareness and get more retweets.

Lastly, promoted trends are simply what they sound. They are hashtags or topics that appear at the top of the section on trending topics. Promoted trends provide your business with an opportunity to create a trending topic. They are especially good if you are trying to create awareness on product launches or upcoming events.

The process of creating a Twitter ad campaign is straightforward and self-explanatory. If you need a bit of guidance, you can check this post that offers a step-by-step tutorial on everything regarding creating an ad on Twitter.

I will conclude this chapter by saying that Twitter is one of the best social media platforms for lead generation. It presents itself as yet another a great tool for researching your audience, engaging with your fans and building the popularity of your brand. This chapter has shown you powerful ways to achieve that. Sure, it involves a lot of work, but if you keep at it, the results will show in due time.

Next, we move on to discuss how you can use LinkedIn to grow your business.

GROWING YOUR BUSINESS USING LINKEDIN

Another great platform that should get your attention is LinkedIn, which prides itself as the ultimate social networking website for professionals. Reid Hoffman, Konstantin Guericke, Jean Luc Vaillant, Allen Blue, and Eric Ly, launched the website in 2003. Microsoft Corporation later bought it in 2016 for $26.2 billion.

LinkedIn has approximately 500 million users. LinkedIn was designed primarily to help job seekers meet new potential employers. Recently, the site has started being used for business as well. It is helping businesses acquire great human resources, build strong relationships with clients, customers, and even partners.

If used well, LinkedIn can benefit your business greatly. In this chapter, we will talk about different strategies that you can use to grow your business through LinkedIn. Let's begin.

Strategy 1: Create a LinkedIn Page

Just like in Facebook, LinkedIn also offers a page as one of its most powerful tools. A LinkedIn page is meant to help other people know more about your business, brand, products or services and job offerings. As such, it is the first place you should start, if you plan to utilize LinkedIn as a way of growing your business.

The process of creating a LinkedIn page is not a difficult task. You will first need to create a LinkedIn profile. Just head over to the company website www.linkedin.com, click on sign up and follow the steps that will be provided. After that, you can read this tutorial created by LinkedIn itself for guidance on how to create a company page.

If you want to get the best out of your company page, it helps to keep the following things in mind:

- Make sure you include your company or business logo as the profile image. According to LinkedIn, company pages with profile picture are six times more likely to get visitors than those that do not. LinkedIn recommends PNG images with dimensions of 300 by 300 pixels. The image should also not be larger than 8 megabytes.

- There are no hard-and-fast rules when it comes to the profile banner. Anything creative that comes to mind is acceptable. You could try communicating offers, company events, a slogan, or an upcoming product launch.

- Make sure you have an "About us" section that is compelling. This is the part that tells people everything there is to know about your company, so you should spend a decent amount of time here. They must have written a great guide that includes sample templates to help you create an "About us" section that stands out.

- Create showcase pages. While company pages are somewhat static and offer general information about your company, showcase pages are dynamic and more interactive. Simply put, a showcase page is a branch of a company page. Here, you can post regular content like new products, ongoing events, charity efforts, and sponsorships. You will need to constantly update the content here. Read this to learn how to create a showcase page.

- Post content that is visually appealing. This means that your communication should not entirely be text-based. You could try throwing in a mixture of nice-looking images as well as videos in your posts. We will talk about sharing great content in the next section.

- Engage your followers by posting thought-provoking questions. Make sure you follow up on their comments and engage them even more.

Strategy 2: Share Great Content

As always, content is king. One of the best ways to promote your business and get more followers on any social media platform is to share great content. In this section, we will talk about the best types of content to share on LinkedIn for the benefit of your business. They include:

1. Blog posts

If you run a blog of any kind, you can share the posts on LinkedIn so that you get more readerships, increase awareness of your brand and get more following. This is especially true if you can share how-to and list-style content.

When sharing blog posts on LinkedIn, be sure to include a great thumbnail, shorten the URL using bitly.com or a similar service and include a comment before introducing the post.

2. Industry news and research

LinkedIn is a platform that is more professional and business-like. Therefore, users are more interested in news and developments occurring in their industry. Therefore sharing content like case studies, reports and white papers on this platform is another great way to engage your followers.

3. Photo updates

Apart from displaying a high level of professionalism and business ethics, it is crucial that you also display a human element. After all, LinkedIn is a social media platform too. One of the best ways to do that is by sharing photos on your showcase pages.

When discussing Twitter, we talked about the importance of multimedia content in creating user engagement. The same is true for LinkedIn. You can post photos of your company employees, activities, events, products and anything that is related to your business. Once again, ensure that you share photos that are visually appealing.

4. Video posts

Video is currently the crystal ball of engagement on social media right now. One mistake that you should never make is to leave out video as part of your content strategy. If you do that, you could miss a lot of opportunities. Read this post for step-by-step instructions on how to post a video on LinkedIn.

If you want to get the best out of videos that you post on LinkedIn, you could try the following ideas:

- Make a video depicting how a day at the place of work looks like.

- You could try interviewing any one of your employees on career tips or their latest project.

- Create a behind-the-scenes video of an event you hosted.

- Create a small product demo or tutorial.

- Post a video of customer testimonials

Strategy 3: Use LinkedIn Ads

For a long time, LinkedIn ads have not received a lot of attention. This is due to the competition from highly effective ad networks like Facebook, Google, and Instagram. However, in recent times, that has changed.

LinkedIn has made great improvements to their platform by introducing features like targeting, conversion tracking and sponsored Inmail. This has made LinkedIn ads more robust and effective.

LinkedIn Ads would work best for you, especially if you run a business that belongs in the B2B (Business-to-Business) sphere. This includes businesses like software companies, manufacturers, and individuals who sell services like consulting, coaching and the like. Also, if you are in a niche that has something to do with skill-building, enhancing professional skills or self-improvement, then you have a go ahead.

Not every business should advertise on LinkedIn though. For instance, companies that sell directly to consumers should generally stay away from LinkedIn ads. This is because the audience on LinkedIn tends to be very professional and business oriented. Failure to follow this advice could lead to wastage of time, money and effort.

LinkedIn ads work in two main ways: Self-service ads and managed campaigns. You set up self-service ads; you manage everything from ad copy, budget and conversion tracking. With managed ads, you task a professional team on LinkedIn to do the work for you.

With that said, let us take a look at the types of ads offered by LinkedIn:

1. Text Ads

As a beginner, you should use these types of ads most. This is because they are the easiest to set up, manage and are more budget-friendly. They typically appear on the right sidebar or the bottom of a page. They are great for creating brand awareness. You can pay for them on either a click or impression basis.

They are typically made up of a headline, an ad copy, an image, and a destination URL.

2. Sponsored Content

These ones typically appear on the homepage where the newsfeed of your target audience is. Unlike text ads, this type of ad offers the opportunity of engagement. Prospects can comment and even share this type of ad.

The parts that make up this ad are an introduction, a headline, a description, and an image. They are used to promote shared content, drive traffic to landing pages and promote company updates. That means you can use them for lead generation.

They too are billed on either a click or impression basis.

3. Sponsored In-mail

This is a unique type of ad that delivers a message that is personalized to LinkedIn's messenger. As such, they end up in the targeted user's inbox. They are made up of your first and last names, a subject line, a summary and profile image.

This type of ad is good for promoting targeted downloads, products, services, registrations to webinars, and live events. They are billed on a cost per-send basis. This means you pay for the number of people you send the message to.□

Creating a LinkedIn campaign is not a difficult thing to do so I won't cover that. You can read this post by LinkedIn, which will walk you through every step of creating any type of ad campaign, including how to use the campaign manager.

In conclusion, using LinkedIn is a great way to grow your business, especially if it is a B2B type of business or one that focuses on highly professional stuff. Whether you are looking to generate more leads, hire competent staff, build awareness or create partnerships, LinkedIn is the way to go. Actually, if you are not using it, you are seriously selling yourself short.

Let us now look at how Snapchat can be used.

GROWING YOUR BUSINESS USING SNAPCHAT

Another social media platform that is of inestimable value to your business is Snapchat.

Evan Spiegel and Bobby Murphy launched Snapchat in 2011. Just like Instagram, it was originally created for the IOS platform. Back then, it was called Picaboo, and the original concept was to have an app that photos could be posted on, that would disappear afterward. Later on that year, it was rebranded to Snapchat.

The Android version was launched in 2012 and that is when the platform really took off. After adding several features over the years, Snapchat today is an app that allows both one-on-one and group chatting whereby people send each other photos, videos and messages that disappear after a short while. Other features of the app are stories, memories, and stickers.

According to the last quarter of 2017, Snapchat reported having approximately 187 million daily users. With traffic like that, you cannot afford to turn a blind eye to it, as this could have a massive impact on your business.

If you have never used Snapchat before, you may feel intimidated to use it. The goal of this chapter is to show you how to use three powerful strategies to build an awesome online presence and promote your business on Snapchat.

Let's begin.

Strategy 1: Post-Great Image Content☐

The first strategy that you can use to promote your business on Snapchat is through great image content. Snapchat is in many ways similar to Instagram. One of the similarities they share is the popularity of image content on the platforms.

However, before you can do anything, you will first need to create a Snapchat account. This is quite easy. You just download the app from either Apple's "App Store" or Google's "Play Store". Once you download and install the app on your phone, you will receive a prompt to sign up once you open the app. Simply follow the prompts and you will have an account. Just remember to use the name of your business as your username.

At this point, you will be free to post anything you feel like on the platform. I would recommend that you do posts on the story section. Posts on the story section typically last for 24 hours. Unlike the regular snaps that disappear within 10 seconds of posting, stories last for longer allowing you to get a decent number of viewers for your content and therefore increasing your chances of building up a huge following.

It would be great if you posted photos of your products, events that you are organizing, your company employees, products that are on offer and just about anything else that comes to mind that may capture the interest of viewers. Just like on Instagram, make sure that your images are of high quality and are edited using Snapchat's filters.

Strategy 2: Post Video Content

The next strategy that should be on your mind is to post video content. Up until this point, I have emphasized the importance of using videos on every social media platform that we have discussed so far. I shall continue to emphasize it for as long as I feel is necessary. Whenever you get the chance to, make sure you share video content. People on social media just love it.

Once again, I would recommend sharing your video content in the story section. Here, they get the best chance of getting a high number of viewers. For ideas on what type of video content, you can try the following:

- Post a video showing whatever happens in your day-to-day operations in business. Fans are always curious about how a typical day in business looks like so show it to them.

- Create a video of what is happening in a live event. Something that is happening life is always more exciting to people and you could get even more viewers.

- Create a behind-the-scenes type of video on your business. You could show how production happens at the place of business.

- You could post a video of other users offering testimonials. Testimonials create more trust in your brand and could increase the number of people who purchase from you.

- You could showcase a new product launch. People are always excited about new product launches. Promoting it on Snapchat is a great way to make the launch even more successful as more people could end up ordering.

It doesn't stop here. Anything that comes to mind that sounds amazing should be a great idea. Marketing on social media is all about carrying out experiments and seeing what works. Use that rule to see what works even better at creating more engagement and thereby more followers.

Strategy 3: Use Snapchat ads

As always, almost every social media platform today provides an option for ads, and for good reasons. Ads are a great way of boosting your efforts and reach, just in case you are new and want results fast.

For instance, a killer ad can get you a huge number of followers or even lead to an increase in sales of a product. Also, ads give you the option of targeting a specific audience which has proven to work very well for businesses, since they see an increase in conversions.

Snapchat offers the following types of ads on its advertising platform:

1. Snap ads

These are the easiest type of ads to set up and are ideal if you run a small to medium enterprise. They are essentially 10-second videos that appear in the story section of Snapchat. They are good for generating user engagement and brand awareness since they blend in well with other stories and therefore feel more like content to the viewer.

2. Sponsored lenses

These types of ads implement the widely used lens feature that Snapchat users love. A lens is like a filter of sorts. They are used to animate a video or photo within the Snapchat platform. They are different from filters in that they are used at the time of taking a photo or video with Snapchat. Filters are used to add special effects to a photo or video afterward. If you create an ad with a well-known or controversial type of lens, you may create a lot of engagement with it.

3. Sponsored Geofilters

These are filters that are specific to a geographic location. They are good for creating brand awareness. This type of ad, along with sponsored lenses, tends to be very costly and is mostly available to companies with deep pockets. For instance, a sponsored Geofilter can cost as much as $100,000! If budget is a concern for you, these ads are not within your reach.

However, custom created Geofilters can be much cheaper, costing as little as $5. Creating Snapchat ads is a simple but comprehensive process. However, covering how to create Snapchat ads in detail is beyond the scope of this book. You can check out this helpful tutorial by Bufferapp. It covers everything from start to finish regarding Snapchat advertising, along with some really helpful tips on how to make the best of them.

While Snapchat may still have a long way to go in terms of things like its advertising platform, it does offer plenty of opportunities to acquire a huge following and grow awareness for your brand, if you are the type who ventures where many do not bother to go. For the most part, Snapchat is still untapped territory for most businesses and marketers.

It may be ideal if you went in and got a piece of the action before the real competition steps in, in the near future.

Lastly, we will focus on Pinterest and how it can be used to boot your business.

GROWING YOUR BUSINESS USING PINTEREST

Pinterest is among the world's leading platforms for sharing ideas and getting inspiration. It may not enjoy as much popularity as other giants like Facebook, Instagram, and Snapchat, but there is a lot of value you can get from it if you use it the right way. This chapter will teach you how to use Pinterest to build a huge following and generate quality traffic for your online business.

Ben Silberman, Evan Sharp, and Paul Sciarra formally launched Pinterest in 2010. The platform allows you to curate content, view and share with others information that you find to be useful and interesting.

As of September 2017, the number of monthly users on Pinterest was estimated to be around 200 million. This is a far cry from the mind-blowing traffic that other popular platforms get. However, this number is still huge enough to warrant your attention.

We will cover four main strategies that you can use on this platform and still do very well.

Strategy 1: Create A Well-Optimized Pinterest Page

Similar to other social media platforms, the best way to create a strong presence is to begin by signing up and creating a complete and well-optimized profile. When people visit your Pinterest page, they will want to know everything they can about your business just by going through your page. If you do not take care of the details about your page, you may just end up losing a lot of prospects just because you did not make a good first impression.

If you do not already have an account on Pinterest, you can create one at business.pinterest.com. This platform will allow you to, among other things, create a business page and do things like advertising on Pinterest. If you have a personal Pinterest account, you can convert your personal page to a business page. Read here for instructions on how to do this.

Some things you need to keep in mind as you create your business page include the following:

- Make sure you include your logo as your profile image. People tend to take pages that have a profile image more seriously than those that don't. On top of that, they help promote the awareness of your brand.
- Make sure you take your time to craft a great "About" section. This is more like a summary of what you do and what you offer, all in 200 words or less. This is also the part that search engines will crawl and offer in their results when people search about you.
- Make sure you list the name of your business or brand instead of your profile name.
- Make sure you include the URL of your website if you have one. This provides a clickable link on your page. This can help Pinterest direct viewers to your website hence increasing traffic and conversions.
- Add a descriptive call to action link on your page which when clicked can perform an action such as take the visitor to your website or a landing page.

Strategy 2: Post-Great Content From Your Blog□

As always, great engaging content always works. If you run a blog that regularly posts content, then you are headed in the direction. Pinterest will offer you a channel for advertising your posts to the world and get more followers. In fact, Pinterest works as a microblogging platform in this way. It is much like Twitter.□

Content can be posted on the platform on what is called boards. A board is a way to group or categorize the type of content (pins) that you share. Pinterest users can either follow you as a user or your boards. You can create boards and share pins like:

- News about your company
- Your blog posts
- Product launches
- Events that your company has organized
- Images and inspiring quotes
- Favorite content that you find on the platform

One more thing, Pinterest users favor visual content more than anything. Therefore, if you want more engagement on your content, you have to present it with great images. Also, add keywords to your image file names and descriptions. This is so that your content can show up whenever people search for your type of content. Also, include a link to the pin so that it directs people to your website

Strategy 3: Post Video Content

The popularity of video content is on the rise and it is affecting every social media platform. This includes Pinterest. Creating video content as part of brand promotion strategy is an incredibly smart move. Pinterest offers the option of creating video pins, which specifically shares video content.

There are a number of ways to share video content on the platform. You can either use the native player within Pinterest or direct users to sites like YouTube or Vimeo. If you decide to upload your videos directly to the platform, make sure that they are in either .mp4 or .mov format. They should also have a minimum length of 4 seconds and a maximum of 30 minutes. Maximum size is 2 gigabytes

To get the best out of your videos, follow these tips:

- Create a captivating introduction so that it prompts your viewers to continue watching it.
- Add a watermark to your videos so that it enhances brand awareness.
- Make sure the content is interesting to your audience. You can try how-to content, interviews, behind-the-scenes, stories or product demos.
- Add music to your videos to give them a special feel.
- Make sure the text in the videos has a good balance.

Strategy 4: Use Pinterest Ads

All social media platforms thrive on ad revenue so you won't find any without an ad program- this includes Pinterest. This section will discuss using ads on the Pinterest platform.

Pinterest offers the following types of ads:

Promoted pins

A promoted pin is essentially a regular pin, only that is has been paid for in order to reach a wider audience. The other difference is that promoted pins have a "Promoted" label at the bottom.

One advantage of this type is that when a user adds the pin to their board, they stop displaying the "Promoted" label and become organic. Also, the traffic and the views they generate after being shared doesn't cost you. They are mostly good for generating traffic.

1. Promoted Video Pins

As the name suggests, these pins display video content. They too have a "Promoted" label that disappears after being shared. They can appear in the news feed, search results and "More like this" section. They play automatically and are good for showcasing products and generating brand awareness.

2. One-tap pins

This is a special type of ad. For one, they look like a typical pin. The only difference is the event that is triggered when they are clicked. The normal behavior of a pin, when clicked, is to open up a more detailed page of the pin itself. When one-tap pins are clicked, they redirect the user to the website that they were linked to.

As such, they are perfect for driving traffic to landing pages where people can sign up for newsletters or purchase an item.

3. Promoted app pins

This type of ad is built for app developers and software companies. If you want traffic that will lead to more installations of your app, this is the perfect way to go. They typically contain an icon of your app, along with an install button. Furthermore, they can be configured to allow installation directly from within Pinterest, without having to redirect users to a website or an app store.

4. Cinematic pins

This type of ad looks and is implemented in the same way as promoted video pins. The only difference is the instances in which the video plays. The video plays when a user scrolls past it and stop playing when a user stops scrolling.

Now that you are in the know about the type of ads offered by Pinterest, you can move on to creating them. The process of creating a Pinterest campaign has been documented in various places all over the internet. There are plenty of guides out there to guide you through. One great guide is this one from the company Pinterest itself. It will take you through the entire process of creating an ad campaign for each type of ad, as well as how to use the ad manager.

In general, if you want to get the most out of your Pinterest ads, follow these guidelines:

- Make sure you create a highly targeted campaign. Pinterest offers you parameters to define your intended audience such as location, age, language, device, gender and much more. The more targeted your audience, the higher the chances of your ad converting.

- Include the right keywords in your campaign. Keywords are the words that people use to search for your content. Researching the right keywords and including them in your ad increases the chances of your ad showing up to the right audience, who will then click on it.

- Make sure your images are of high quality and attractive. Since Pinterest is very visual based, it, therefore, means that the most eye-catching visuals get the most attention. Spend some time looking for a great looking image and you can bet that your ad will convert better.

- Add a call to actions to your ads. Adding a call to action prompts users to take the next step and this has been known to make ads convert better than those that don't. For instance, a message like "Get it here now" will work better than one without it.

- Also, make sure you time your campaigns. Targeting periods when your audience is likely to be more active can really work in your favor and help your ads get higher conversion rates. For instance, events like Christmas, Black Friday, Easter, Valentine's day, Mother's day and the like can really work well especially if you deliver the message strategically.

In conclusion, utilizing Pinterest is a great, simple and highly affordable way to promote your business online and increase its visibility as well as its customer base. This is so especially because the platform has less competition from other marketers at the moment. If you patiently implement the strategies covered in this chapter, you will slowly start reaping great benefits from the platform that will only grow with time.

CONCLUSION

I want to commend you for reading this far. It communicates a real passion and commitment to learning how to tap into the amazing power of social media. In this digital age that we live in today, social media is one of the most powerful tools in an entrepreneur's arsenal. This book has served the purpose of showing you how to quickly get started with this amazing tool.

I will not go ahead and make an outrageous claim that this book has covered social media in its entire entirety. That would be snake oil salesmanship. But I am confident to say that it's a good start. There are several pieces out there in cyberspace. Becoming good at harnessing social media is an art and mastering that art takes time and effort.

If you become more diligent in your search, it will be only a matter of time before you strike gold.

Thank you for choosing to purchase this book and I hope it becomes of great value to you.

If you found the book valuable, can you recommend it to others? One way to do that is to post a review on Amazon.

Thank you and good luck!

ERNIE BRAVEBOY

YOUTUBE CHANNEL SUCCESS

HOW TO CREATE A GREAT YOUTUBE CHANNEL, GAIN MILLIONS OF SUBSCRIBERS, AND MAKE MONEY TOO

BY

ERNIE BRAVEBOY

INTRODUCTION

I want to thank you and congratulate you for buying the book, **"YouTube Channel Success:** How To Create A Great YouTube Channel, Gain Million Of Subscribers, And Make Money Too."

Today, thanks to YouTube, anyone can be an influential media personality. YouTube is so potent a platform that other than the billions of people visiting the platform every day, it is also making many others millionaires.

Take the example of Daniel Middleton (DanTDM). His YouTube channel, a channel dedicated to video games, and that has over 19.8 million subscribers and well over 13.3 billion total video views, earns him upwards of $16.5 million annually, and he is not the only one. Evan Fong, Dude Perfect, PewDiePie, Smosh and Ryan ToysReview, and many other YouTubers generate millions of dollars off YouTube annually.

While we are not saying you will generate millions of dollars from YouTube, by creating an amazing YouTube channel populated with amazing content that people love to watch whether, for their education or entertainment, you can create a YouTube channel that has millions of subscribers and that generates passive income. This guide is going to show you among other things:

How to get started with YouTube (everything you need to know to get started),

1. How to grow your channel exponentially so that it has millions of followers,

2. How to increase traffic to your YouTube channel,

3. How to monetize your YouTube channel using the most effective monetization strategies as well as tons of other YouTube stuff that will get you ready for YouTube stardom:

Thanks again for buying this book. I hope you enjoy it!

SECTION 1: LAYING THE FOUNDATION

To create an amazing YouTube channel that attracts a loyal following, you need to lay a proper foundation because this foundation is the rock upon which you will build your YouTube Empire.

Most of the content in this section will be beginner geared in the sense that it will outline all the various elements you need to have in place to position your YouTube channel for maximum success.

GETTING STARTED WITH YOUTUBE: WHY YOUTUBE?

If you are new to creating a YouTube channel, the first thing you are likely to ask yourself is, why YouTube? Why should you bother to create a YouTube channel or become a YouTube personality? Well, this short chapter is going to cover that by showing you some of the ways through which YouTube can enrich your life.

Video is the future

First off, as a society, we are gravitating more towards video content. Think about it. Whenever you visit your Facebook timeline, what are you likely to see more, video post-shares, or text posts? If your Facebook/social media timeline is like that of most people, you are likely to see more video posts/shares. This is because video content is the future. YouTube is the mother of all video platforms.

Whether you want to establish a social brand or any form of business, you will have to leverage the power of viral video marketing to grow your business. You should start a great YouTube channel because when you have one, you can easily share your amazing videos to your social media channels (thereby driving more traffic to the channel), and even easily embed the video content into your text/blog content.

Did you know that in any given month, 8 out of 10 people aged 18-49 watch YouTube videos? Did you also know that in any given hour, YouTube users upload more than 400 hours of video content?

What does this tell you? It should tell you that, no matter how you look at it, video content is the way to go. In fact, in the present environment, instead of starting a blog (you should still consider starting one); you should consider starting a YouTube channel and using it as your primary communication method with your chosen audience.

The power of video marketing

The power of video marketing is the other reason why you should consider starting a YouTube channel.

Because they are easy to absorb, videos, especially short and sweet ones that have a purpose—whether that purpose is entertainment or education—videos are easy to share on social media and other platforms. It is actually common for video shares to outdo text share, especially on social media.

When you create great videos, videos that your audience find valuable, they are likely to share the videos with their audiences who are then likely to share the video with their audiences or friend's list.

The effect of this is that in the end, your 2-3 minutes video can go viral and within a short time.

What does this mean?

It means that if you create great videos, videos that look professional and that fulfill a need, you do not have to dedicate too much time to marketing: your videos will simply market themselves because users will want to share the value in them.

The money

We cannot fail to mention the money aspect. YouTube is an amazing way to generate passive income, an income that does not require your active time and energy input to continue trickling into your bank account.

Think of it this way.

YouTube is a content platform. Like a blog, once you publish a YouTube video, it is always available to all users interested in the topic covered by the video—to make sure users find your videos, you have to optimize your videos with keywords, something we shall talk about later. This means that if you create a viral video, a video that users want to view and share, and then monetize it, you can generate tons of dollars in passive income all without ever having to do anything other than uploading the video and engage in the initial marketing.

In the introductory part of this guide, we illustrated how thousands of YouTubers are leveraging YouTube to generate millions of dollars in revenue. These individuals are now so popular that their names are household brands in their chosen niche/industry.

If you create an amazing YouTube channel, you too can generate thousands if not millions of dollars in passive income each month. Before you can do that, however, you first need to choose your niche/topic of concentration. The next chapter talks about that.

THE RICHES ARE IN THE NICHES: WHY AND HOW TO CHOOSE A NICHE FOR YOUR YOUTUBE CHANNEL

A niche is a segment of a market or in this case, the topic of your YouTube channel. The reasons why you should choose a niche are as many as the sands of the ocean.

For the purpose of this guide, we shall restrict ourselves to very specific reasons that illuminate why, before you start creating your YouTube channel, you should dedicate a fair amount of time and thought to the topic of your channel.

Why Choosing A Niche Is So Important

First, as implied, a niche is a segment of a market or in simpler terms, we can define it as a smaller topic in a larger one. For instance, health is a general topic. Under it are smaller topics such as weight loss, the various diet plans, exercise, and many others. The same applies to many other topics: we have one main, umbrella topic under which we find many other smaller topics.

The title of this chapter reads something along "the riches are in the niche." No truer words exist. Part of the reason why the riches are in the niches has to do with targeting. When your approach to marketing is too broad—remember that to grow your YouTube channel to millions of views and subscribers, you will have to market it—your marketing strategy will have a weak bite and you will not get value for money. Think of it this way.

If you decide to target the general health and beauty category under which we find other categories such as tanning, cellulite treatment, facials, acne care, etc., your marketing strategy will be all over the place because you will be attempting to target different audiences that have different needs, desires, and wants.

On the other hand, if you choose to concentrate on acne care, for example, a niche or sub-category of the main category, your marketing plan is likely to be very effective because you will be endeavoring to fulfill the needs and desires of a targeted audience that want a specific outcome.

This simple explanation is why you should niche down. If you would like to learn a bit more about why the riches are in the niche—and covertly, why you should only start your YouTube channel after choosing a niche—you can read more at https://medium.com/multiplier-magazine/the-riches-are-in-the-niches-209dd235e3d8.

Now that you know that, let us discuss the process by which you can choose a niche for your YouTube channel:

Tips And Strategies For Choosing A Niche For Your YouTube Channel

You now know that without choosing your niche—and doing so diligently enough—you are likely to create a YouTube channel that sees minimal growth, views, and subscription (sometimes zero), and therefore, one that does not reward—by generating a passive income that can run into millions—all the hard work you do to create videos for YouTube.

When it comes to choosing a niche (for your YouTube channel, Blog, or whatever else—including business—), you should only have one thing in mind and that is to *choose a niche where you know you can provide immense value to a dedicated target audience.*

If you look at the most successful businesses (maintaining a YouTube channel is a lot like running a business—only a fun one—), you will note that most of them are successful because they offer their audiences immense value.

If you get into a niche where you do not provide value, you will fail to attract an audience, and, only by attracting an audience that loves your YouTube content can you grow what we can only call a successful YouTube business that has millions of subscribers and that pays you well.

To determine if you can give your target audiences the immense value they desire, you should follow but one rule: think of a topic that interests you—hobbies—or one that you would passionately like to learn more about. This can be anything; the galaxy, a new language, coding, web design, makeup, or whatever else you can imagine—and then determine if there are other people out there in the world that would love the content on the same topic.

An ideal niche is one where you create content, video or otherwise—in this case, video—on topics that excite you or you are passionate about and that have a ready audience. How do you determine if a niche has a ready audience?

You can do so in one of two ways. First, you can create a buyer persona, or you can use a Keyword research tool to determine how many people are using Google and other search engines to search for similar content. The two methods can work individually but work better when combined.

Here are the steps to follow to use both methods—individually and together—

Step 1: Create a list

Think of the topics you would like to create video content for YouTube on. As we said earlier, this can be anything; poetry, how to draw, how to learn X or Y, etc. Think of 10-50 topics. Do not worry, if you allow yourself a few minutes of quiet and creative thinking, you will come up with a healthy list of ideas.

Once you have your list, look it over and out of the ideas you have, circle 10 that inspire you the most, the ones that when you think of creating content on, ignite a spark of joy within you.

Buyer Persona

Now that you have your list of 10, think a little about the type of person that would be interested in the same type of online content. What is that person's age? Where is that person (in terms of geo-location)? What does that person do? What are his or her main interests and do they relate to your niche? What type of content is that person likely to absorb online?

In marketing, we call this creating a buyer persona. A buyer person helps you create a clear mental image of the type of persona that would be interested in the type of content you would like to create.

You can create a buyer persona online using tools such as Xtensio.

After creating a buyer persona for each of the 5 to 10 of your passion topics/niche, you now need to determine if that niche has a potential audience or simply put if the person you have described in your buyer persona is actually looking for relevant content on the niche.

Step 2: Research niche profitability

Niches/topics that have a low volume traffic quantity, which means that not that many people are looking for related content, will not perform well or help you generate millions of followers or a passive income.

To research the profitability of a niche, you can use a Keyword research tool. Start by asking yourself, "When this audience goes online, what type of content is he or she looking for?" Then using these metrics, come up with a list of at least 50 words that the person would type into his or her search box when looking for content on your intended topic.

An easy way to determine the type of content people are searching for on Google and other search engines are to head to your search bar and typing the same words in. For instance, if after looking over our list, we determine that we would like to create a YouTube channel dedicated to home cooking, we can postulate that the person typing such words into YouTube (YouTube runs on Google Search engine) is most likely looking for recipes.

If we head to YouTube and type a recipe, something like "pumpkin pie," these platforms will auto-populate the rest to show you what people are typing into the search bar:

YOUTUBE

pumpkin pie red
pumpkin pie recipe
pumpkin pie recipe from scratch
pumpkin pie recipe easy
pumpkin pie recipe with real pumpkin
pumpkin pie recipe minecraft
pumpkin pie recipe allrecipes
pumpkin pie recipe vegan
pumpkin pie recipe martha stewart

GOOGLE

best pumpkin pie

best pumpkin pie **recipe**
best pumpkin pie **in atlanta**
best pumpkin pie **from scratch**
best pumpkin pie **crust**
best pumpkin pie **cheesecake recipe**

From the above, we can see that creating a video on "how to create a pumpkin pie from scratch" means we shall have an audience because YouTube has shown us that people are typing those words into their search bars.

While this is great, on the back end, it may be that only 10 people (out of a world that has over 3.5 billion internet users) are typing those words into their search bars; enter a keyword research tool.

A keyword research is a tool used by online marketers to determine how many people are typing specific words into their search engine bars. The more people typing specific keywords into their search engines, the more likely you are to have a potentially profitable niche.

To determine how many users are typing specific keywords into their search boxes—we4 call this average monthly searches or AMS can use a free keyword research tool such as Google Keyword Planner or a paid one such as AHREF.

For instance, when we type pumpkin pie into Google keyword planner, we can see the following results from which we can see that the terms "easy pumpkin pie recipe" have 1,000 to 10,000 monthly searches. This means that 1-10k people are typing these exact keywords into their search boxes, which means that, if we create a video on the same, assuming we do a great job of creating amazing content and optimizing it for search engines, we can get over 10,000 views on our "easy pumpkin pie recipe" YouTube video.

Keyword (by relevance)	Avg. monthly searches ?	Competition ?	Suggested bid ?	Ad impr. sh	Add to plan
easy pumpkin pie recipe	1K – 10K	Low	$1.84		»
easy pumpkin pie	1K – 10K	Low	$0.67		»
pumpkin pie recipe easy	1K – 10K	Low	$0.76		»
easy recipe for pumpkin pie	100 – 1K	Medium	$0.78		»
pumpkin pie easy recipe	100 – 1K	Low	$1.80		»
recipe for easy pumpkin pie	10 – 100	Low	$0.62		»

The goal of keyword research is to help you pursue a niche that has a potential high traffic volume. Choose to go into your preferred niche only if it has an average monthly search of 1-10k; choosing a niche whose main topics see 10-100 monthly searches is why most people create YouTube channels that flop and fail to take off.

Take your list of possible niches through this process and use the information you gather to choose a niche that fills you with passion and whose content on the same has a ready target audience.

In some instances, after taking your list of possible niches through this process, you may determine that your intended niche, the one that fills you with the most creative passion—remember that creating viral videos for YouTube requires tons of creativity—lacks a high search volume.

If that is the case, think of your main goal: what do you want your YouTube video content to achieve? Once you have this, simply think of the type of person that would want to view or that content. The buyer person you create from this will greatly help you determine which words such a person is likely to type when searching for content on YouTube or Google.

You can learn more about choosing a niche for your YouTube channel from https://medium.com/@diana_21435/how-to-choose-the-best-niche-for-your-youtube-channel-2e0fb5f465b0

This https://toughnickel.com/self-employment/10-Most-Profitable-YouTube-Niche-Ideas outlines a list of the 10 most popular YouTube niches (you can use it for inspiration)

Now that you have one or two topics that have proven to have a healthy traffic potential (and align with your passions), the next part is to create your YouTube channel and start populating it with valuable content that will thrill your audiences.

The next chapter talks in brief about how to set up your YouTube channel fast.

SETTING UP: CREATING YOUR YOUTUBE CHANNEL FAST

As suggested by the title of the chapter, this chapter seeks to help you create your YouTube channel as fast as possible. When we say set up, what we are actually talking about is creating the backbone of your channel in a way that sets you up for massive success.

Let us get started:

Setting up your YouTube channel is an easy feat. All you have to do is sign up for one using your Google account (Gmail account really). You can even use the same Google mail (Gmail) address to register multiple YouTube channels, which should prove very effective.

After creating your Google account (if you don't have one; if you do, all you have to do is sign in), Head over to YouTube—the homepage, which you can find on the link below—and from there, navigate to your account, which should be a thumbnail of your picture on the top right corner of your browser page.

Doing this will call up a drop-down menu; from there, you can choose to go to your Creator Studio, which is essentially the backend of your YouTube channel or create one if you have not. Clicking the creator studio should bring you to the following page:

From there, the process of creating a YouTube channel is very straightforward and easy. To ensure that you go through this process in a way that prepares your channel for massive success, you ought to pay attention to specific elements the most important of which we shall now discuss:

Important Elements To Pay Attention To When Creating Your Successful YouTube Brand

The first and perhaps the most important thing you should pay special attention to is the name. Your YouTube name is your first audience contact point. Make sure the name is representative of your YouTube channel brand; make it memorable.

You can choose a YouTube channel name based on your niche, i.e. if you are in the makeup niche, you can name your channel based on this, or you can come up with a creative, memorable name.

Take the example of PewDiePie (read Pie-Die-Pie), a channel primarily in the gaming niche. The proprietor of the channel, Felix

Arvid Ulf Kjellberg, says the name is creative the 'pew' in the name is the sound made by laser guns in video games while the "die" part means what happens after someone fires a laser gun: death (in the video game).

A great YouTube name will make it easier to brand your YouTube enterprise.

The other thing you want to pay attention to is the style. Here, you will want to concentrate on your overall outlay, your channel art including channel image and profile picture, how you organize your content, your channel description, and channel trailer (a video that plays automatically every time someone lands on your channel's homepage).

https://blog.bufferapp.com/create-a-youtube-channel resource has great content on the various elements you need to optimize as well as change (it also shows you exactly how to make those changes).

Once you have optimized the various elements of your new channel, you can then start creating and uploading videos. The next chapter talks about the various tools and equipment you need to shoot amazing video.

NOTE: As you start uploading video, you will note that, initially, YouTube will restrict your content length to less than 15 minutes. To remove this restriction, you need to verify your account as fast as possible so that Google bots can start viewing you as a real person instead of a bot that just creates accounts.

The verification process is easy; once you get to the verification page, all you will need to do is verify your account by inputting into the dialog box the code Google sends to your mobile phone.

Your Essential YouTube Creator Equipment Guide

The amazing thing about being a great YouTube content creator is that, once you have a great topic that inspires you and that has an audience ready to appreciate the value your video content ads to their life—whether that is education (video tutorials) or fun (funny video compilations)—you do not need much to start. Actually, the camera on your smartphone is enough to get you started.

However, since the idea is to create great video content—creating great, valuable content is how you create a successful YouTube channel—you need to go above your smartphone camera: start there yes, but evolve fast.

The following are the bare minimum (the essential) equipment you need to start out fast.

1: Camera

Depending on the nature of your video channel, you can start with a quality webcam. If you have a bit more, you can buy a quality DSLR camera. Only buy a high-end camera after YouTubing for a while (6-12 months is ideal) and verifying that your niche has a ready audience and the potential to grow into a full-time business.

When considering which camera to use, remember that the quality of your videos will also determine its popularity. Do not go for a camera that does not shoot anything below 720P.

2: Tripod

If your camera lacks a tripod, you will need one so that you can shoot steady videos. A tripod will offer you immense flexibility even when you are shooting on your mobile phone (we have tripods for mobile phones).

Nevertheless, tripods are not exactly essential because if you are shooting still video, you can place your camera atop books or other household items—many YouTubers do this.

3: Microphone

If you are in the tutorial or explainer niche, you will need a quality microphone since most of the available cameras—whether DSLR or your iPhone or smartphone—lack a robust microphone.

Get yourself an external microphone that has great sound quality and separates audio recording capabilities so that you can record audios separately and then mix it into the video afterwards for amazing sound.

Microphones can be expensive. Evaluate your microphone needs depending on the type of content you intend to create and move from there.

4: Green screen

A green screen is not essential; still, it comes in very handy when you want a clear background or to add effects to your recording environment. You can DIY a green screen using a sheet and some green dye, or you can buy one for $50 or less.

5: Video capture and audio editing tools

If you will be uploading content captured from your screen, which can be video tutorials, you will need a capable screen capture software. You have plenty of choices; you can use OBS studio, Snagit, CamStudio, or any other capable video capture software.

You will also need to have video editing software of which you have many options depending on your operating system. Before you splurge on expensive video and audio editing software, remember that the creator studio has an in-built video editing suite.

Good video editing software will also have capable audio editing tools to you can use; if that is not the case, or you have recorded your audio separately, you will need a quality audio editor so that you can clean your audio before you mix it with the video.

As your channel grows and generates a passive income, you can then splurge and build a real recording studio for your YouTube business. You can build a low-cost recording studio dedicated to growing your channel. https://www.makeuseof.com/tag/build-low-cost-youtube-studio/ resource talks about what you need to do that (mind you, you should only do this after your channel has grown to a specific point).

At this point in the guide, you should be ready to create great content for your YouTube channel. You should be ready to grow it too. Experiment with your new equipment and shooting a few video content for your channel. Edit and upload the videos as you get your feet wet with using the creator studio.

Now that you have chosen a niche, researched it, and then created great content for your waiting audience, content that adds value to their lives, you are ready to grow your YouTube channel into a thriving brand/business. The chapters in the next section talk about this at length.

Section 2: Growing Your Channel - How To Create A Great YouTube Channel & Gain Millions Of Subscribers

Now that you have laid the foundation upon which your YouTube channel will thrive, you are ready to take it to the next level. At this point, you should be in a position where you are creating videos consistently and can comfortably use the various equipment and tools at your disposal.

How to Create a Great YouTube Channel that Has a Rabid Following and Million of Subscribers

First, to create a great YouTube channel, you should make sure you are in a niche that has the traffic potential so that when you create great video content and then optimize this content for search, you can drive organic traffic to your YouTube videos and channel.

Before we look at the ingredients, you need to create a standout YouTube channel that has a viral following and that earns you money, let us talk about video quality and how it affects your channel's success.

How To Create Videos That Attract Viral Views

YouTube is a search engine. Therefore, to create great content—content is what drives a channel to stardom—you will need to optimize your content and channel in the same way you would optimize a blog.

Once you start creating videos, you will want to improve your video quality as fast as possible because to get more views—more views often lead to a higher subscription—you will need to create quality content and then optimize it for search. We shall shortly discuss how to optimize your video content for search.

If you concentrate on the following three elements/steps, you should create quality video content that attracts viewership and helps you create a loyal following.

1: The purpose of the video

The purpose of the video—what it intends to do; either entertain or educate/accomplish—is at the very heart of how to create great YouTube channel that has quality content and thus, an amazing viewership.

When creating your YouTube content, always keep in mind that the people who will view it will have two main outcomes in mind: entertainment or education. For instance, someone looking for content on how to apply makeup is looking to solve a problem. Make sure that your content accomplishes both or at least one (educational videos with a funny twist or an element of personality are especially popular).

Understating that YouTube viewers (and all online users for that matter) are looking to fulfill these two needs will greatly influence the type of content you create. Aim to create videos that help your users solve their problem or accomplish what they want as first as possible.

This means that, while your videos should have a catchy introduction—perhaps a channel's theme song—you should not drag it out or the problem. Produce to-the-point video content; only by doing so, will see you attract and grow a loyal following as well as YouTube video views.

2: Quality trumps quantity

Common advice is to upload regularly. This is great advice and indeed, frequently uploading new video content is one of the key YouTube success factors.

Nevertheless, always remember that a channel producing and uploading 100, low-quality content per month cannot outmatch one that produces and uploads even 20, extremely high-quality content. This is in line with best SEO practices.

When we talk of quality content, we mean quality in terms of the video content—if it helps the viewers achieve their desired outcome—and quality in terms of how you shoot the videos. To create a great channel, you need to remember that low-quality videos are not how you get there.

A high-quality video is one that looks professionally shot—whether you are shooting from your webcam, YouTube studio or wherever else does not matter, the video has to be of high quality. This kind of video is clear, well lit, and not blurry. It oozes professionalism and s as if someone has truly invested in its quality.

To create such a video, you can use the classic white or green background. Such a background makes your video content look crisp and professional; it keeps the audiences' view focused on you instead of the things in your background. This type of setup is especially ideal for instances where you are shooting presentations of yourself (in-front-of-the-camera shoots).

Depending on your niche and the type of content you create, you can also use a whiteboard video where you narrate video drawings on a whiteboard. Whiteboards are especially great when you are creating explainer videos.

Unlike white background videos that are relatively easy to shoot—you simply need a white background and a nice enough camera placed on a tripod (a good microphone is also essential—

whiteboard videos require special illustration skills. If you lack these skills, you can hire a freelancer.

High-quality videos also feature great editing, which is why video editing software made it to the list of things you will need to set up a successful YouTube business. If you do not know how to edit your videos, you can hire someone. Nevertheless, we will briefly discuss how to edit your YouTube video content.

3: Brandable

Being a YouTube creator is a lot like—at least to some degree—owning a TV show, which is why for a channel to be successful, it needs regular viewership. To create an Amazing video show, you need to make a name for yourself and your YouTube channel. The best way to do this is by uploading video content regularly.

Commit yourself to create, editing, and uploading new video content with some predictable frequency. Make sure that your channel has a great video offering. As you get started, upload new content frequently; doing so will give your channel more SEO juice on YouTube.

Having more videos is also a great chance to attract a healthy viewership as well as grow your subscriber list because even if someone does not like one of your first videos, another video offers you a chance to impress that audience and turn him or her into a subscriber.

As you grow your YouTube channel—, which, inadvertently, grows as you upload more, high-quality videos—your viewership and subscriber list will grow. This growth is not linear. The growth is likely to start low where your videos get minimal views and your subscribers list is as empty as an empty cobbler's curse. Gradually, however, the growth will be exponential especially if you have done a great job at niche selection and producing shareable content.

Because optimizing your YouTube content for search is the best way to increase your YouTube following and grow your YouTube channel (views, subscribers, and even revenue), you must ace this prospect of your YouTube empire. The next chapter of this section shows you how to do just that.

YOUTUBE GROWTH HACKING: OPTIMIZING YOUTUBE CONTENT FOR SEARCH AND IMPROVED VIEWS AND SUBSCRIBERS

Ensuring that your YouTube content generates as many quality views as possible is what turns a YouTube channel into a success. To ensure that your videos are generating views consistently and that your viewers are watching a large portion of your video content, you have to create great videos, which we have already covered how to do, and then optimize this content for search so that your videos appear as the most relevant for your intended keywords.

The general rule of growth hacking your YouTube channel's success is to ensure that your videos generate at least 3,600 views soon after uploading them. To a search engine such as YouTube, the difference between 0 and 2,000 is larger than the difference between 2,000 and 200,000, which means once you clock a few thousand views (over 3,000 views to be precise), you can easily rank first for your intended keywords assuming you optimize all the other SEO factors such as rating and user retention.

Aim to drive at least several thousand views to each video as soon as you upload it; this will ensure your channel rolls on forwarding full steam. How do you get these views as fast as possible? That depends on the nature of your niche and audience. Some effective optimization strategies include:

Cross Promotion

In cross-promotion, you leverage an already existing fan base. This method works best when you have a following—no matter how small—within your chosen niche. Another way to cross promote your channel is to ask other top YouTubers in your niche to host you (you participate in their video) so that you can gain access to their audience; obviously, this prospect works best when you have chosen a valuable contributor within your niche.

At the end of the cross-promotion video, have a call to action asking users of that channel to subscribe to your channel and ensure you have a keyword optimized (specifically optimized for the subject covered by that specific video) link to your channel on the video's description text.

How do you find channels on which you can cross promote? The easiest way to do this is to type your intended keywords—the ones you want to rank for—on YouTube and from the results, monitor the number of views and subscribers a channel has; the higher the subscriber list, the better for you.

After you find several such targets, simply email them with an offer to create valuable video content for their channel (always remember that as long as you provide value to an existing target audience, your YouTube channel will be a success).

Email Marketing

Again, if you have already established yourself as an authority in your niche, perhaps through a blog or social media, you should promote your content to that audience preferably via email—assuming you have in place an effective email collection strategy.

As stated earlier, while you can create YouTube as a standalone business, you are better of coupling it with a blog that allows you to create and post an accompanying blog post for each video you upload. You can then embed the corresponding YouTube video into the blog post for improved SEO juice to your blog as well as YouTube video and channel.

A blog as an accompaniment to your YouTube business is a great way to ensure that you give readers more options. Some will opt to read the blog while others will opt to view the video. In all though, a blog will present you a rare opportunity. It will allow you to entice your audience with a great free offer in exchange for their email addresses, which is only great for your YouTube channel since it means that every time you create new content, you can market to your list to drive tons of views to your videos.

Still, on email marketing, another effective way to drum up more views and subscribers—not to mention optimize your content for search—is to embark on an email outreach campaign. An email outreach campaign simply means creating a list of top bloggers, YouTubers, and Vloggers in your niche, and then asking them to share your high quality, extremely valuable content with their audiences. If you provide immense value to your target audience—and theirs since you are in similar niches—these individuals will be more than likely to oblige you.

As your YouTube channel grows and your views rack up, the subscriber list will grow on automatic as you retain your target through valuable video content. At this point, you can then consider using other promotion strategies such as paid advertising on Google and other platforms such as social media where you use paid advertising to expose your content to a larger audience base.

If you do this, your channel will generate tons of views and subscribers. Once you have this structure in place, you can then

YOUTUBE CHANNEL SUCCESS

move to optimize your channel for search and thereby, improved growth (growth is how you build a YouTube channel that has millions of views and subscribers). Let us talk about the various elements you should optimize.

103

YouTube SEO Hacks: The Important Elements To Optimize

First, you should understand that the quality of your video matters the most. Trying to optimize a bad video is a futile effort. The elements that make a video of high quality are great recording (high-quality video and sound, lighting, etc.), and high-quality content that helps users solve a problem or fulfill a need.

Always remember that at the heart of YouTube success lies in one secret: provide so much value that your target audience has no choice but to take note. Make sure your message—and the mediums you use to communicate it—resonate with your target base.

Once you have that in place, optimize the following elements

NOTE: To optimize your YouTube video content, you will need to perform keyword research. Keywords are an integral part of ranking your YouTube videos first since the YouTube search engine is very similar to Google. The better and more targeted your keywords are, the higher your chances of ranking first, and the more likely you are to grow your channel fast.

For keyword research, you can use a free or paid keyword research tool. You can learn more about keyword research for YouTube https://backlinko.com/hub/youtube/youtube-keyword-research and https://longtailpro.com/keyword-research-for-youtube/.

Once you have your list of keywords, you will want to optimize:

Title

Your intended keywords should appear significantly on your title; this increases visibility and ensures that when users type those exact keywords into YouTube, the search engine matches their search query to your content as the most relevant.

Essentially, ensuring your keywords are in the title of your video means you should dedicate a substantial amount of thought and time to coming up with unique video headlines. The rule of thumb is to make the titles appealing to humans while at the same time making the titles search engines friendly by integrating your keywords into the title.

Meta

Ensure your videos have a human-oriented description that is also keyword rich. Nevertheless, keep in mind that the idea of a Meta description is to help audiences know the nature of the video and therefore, your use of keywords within the Meta description should not compromise this ability. Create keyword optimized Meta descriptions that stir up interest and click through in your audience.

Because the description will appear against each search results, make the description brief, to the point, and where possible without compromising human readability, keyword rich.

Tags

While not compulsory, tags help YouTube associate your video content with text, which means that can greatly improve your video ranking. Use keyword-optimized tags but avoid overdoing it by using irrelevant tags or too many tags.

Video thumbnail

Successful YouTube channels are ones that aim to create a brand by creating a sort of baseline element of their business. On YouTube, the best way to do this, to create a sort of uniformity and therefore, a visually pleasant YouTube channel that is both memorable and enticing to its intended target audience, great, visually pleasing, and optimized-for-your-niche video thumbnails are the best way to do this.

Great thumbnails will give your channel a great aesthetic you want and help you create a brand around your chosen niche. The following screenshot shows the power of video thumbnails on YouTube as a branding and effective marketing tool:

Stand For Something In Your
Content and Leaning On

308 views · 2 months ago

Structuring Video In Your
Business Does Not Fall On

395 views · 4 months ago

How 7-Figure Entrepreneurs
Are Using Video In Their

371 views · 4 months ago

VLOGS   PLAY ALL

Making a 3 Part Video Series
For a Product Launch -

Sold With Video
1.2K views · 2 years ago

Why Do I VLOG on a Video
Marketing Channel? - VLOG

Sold With Video
580 views · 2 years ago

How To Make a Brick Wall
Video Set (DIY) - VLOG #12

Sold With Video
1.8K views · 2 years ago

Image courtesy of <u>*Sold With Video*</u>, *a great YouTube channel that offers great tutorials on how to market your videos.*

The channel has over 34k subscribers (34,127 subscribers to be exact), and most of its video uploads have an average of 1.2k views with some attracting as much as 450k views. That means that, on one specific video, 450,000 people are viewing and actively engaging with his content.

This proves that the channel and the topic it covers has a great viewership that the proprietor of the channel can capitalize on by providing immense value within the niche and then finding easy ways to monetize the channel.

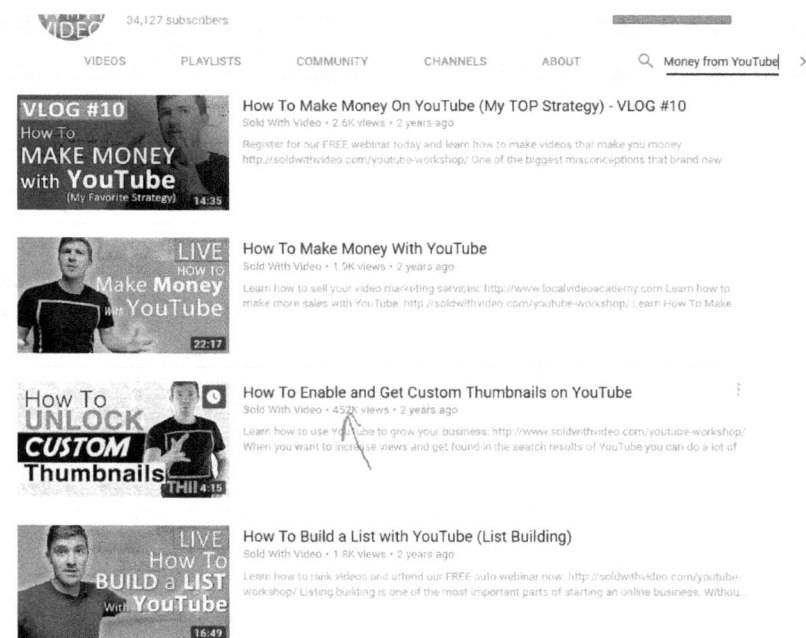

To create thumbnails and therefore a brand around your video content, you can use https://support.google.com/youtube/answer/72431?hl=en resource from Google or watch a video on how to do so https://www.youtube.com/watch?v=Uby_wyOoBQ4.

For great video thumbnails, make the image as large and as light as possible. YouTube recommends that you *"keep your image **1280x720** and upload in image formats such as as.JPG, GIF, BMP, or.PNG."*

You can watch https://www.youtube.com/watch?v=VyToVPBU9Do great video tutorial on how to edit your image easily using free tools.

Closed Captions

YouTube is a video-based search engine. Like Google (the search engine), it depends on information (such as your video titles and their relevance to your niche, name of your channel, the links pointing back to your videos, user interaction with videos, and other metrics), to determine which search results are most relevant to user queries.

When you add closed captions and subtitles to your video content, you give the search ranking bots at Google more signals to relate the nature of your content to its users. Subtitles and CC (closed captions) are also a great way to allow users to interact with your content even when they are in noisy (or even quiet) environments.

Google has a great tutorial on how to add CC and subtitles to your video content:

If you prefer immersive learning (video learning), watch this amazing video by Roberto Blake, a creative entrepreneur whose YouTube channel has a subscriber list of 335k:

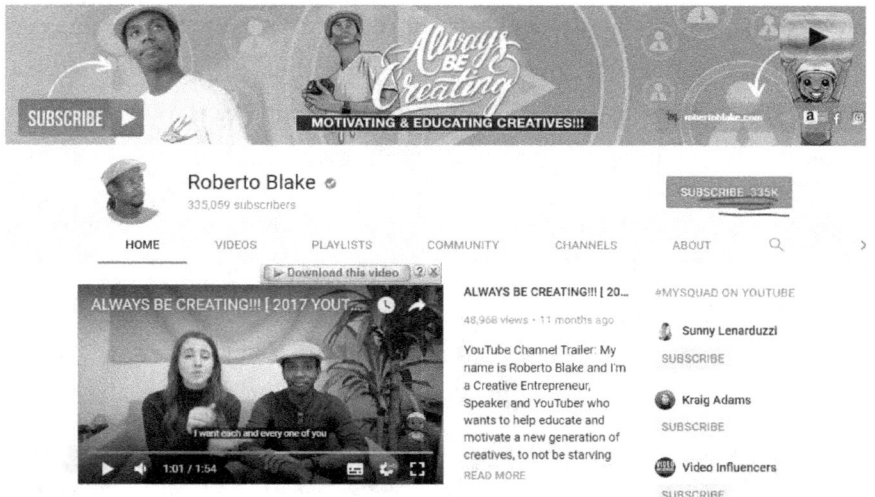

To ensure you are also creating a tribe around your content (doing this is how you become a leader in your industry by proving yourself a valuable contributor within that niche), you make your content—and channel—as interactive as possible.

You can improve your ranking, video views, and even subscription by encouraging your target audience to interact with your Video content, which improves engagement, and by giving you feedback on the value you are offering; interaction with your audience can help you come up with great content ideas.

Improving engagement and interaction is an especially important ranking factor that Google uses to determine the quality and relevance of video content so that it can give its users the best and most relevant search results. The amount of time a YouTube user watches your video is especially important. To improve this, use the first 15 seconds of your video to capture your audience's attention and then build great content from there.

Once you create great content that attracts a viewership, you can then concentrate on building your subscriber list. In most cases, your subscriber's list will start out slow but gain great momentum as you create great engaging content for a ready audience.

Add a Call to Action (CaT) to all your videos as a way to remind your audiences that if they liked the content and found it useful, they should like, comment on, and share your content, and subscribe to your channel for tons of other valuable content on your niche of concentration.

You can see why that'd be effective.

https://youtu.be/LOI_zSR-BPo has a great tutorial on how to overlay a call to action into your videos.

You can also drive up your engagement using an End-screen, the content that plays 5-20 seconds before the end of a video. You can use this segment to promote engagement on your channel (engagement in terms of views, comments, shares across different channels, and even your subscriber list).

https://www.youtube.com/watch?v=GlQEU-LCiV0 video resource will show you how to add an end screen to your videos. If you are great at video editing, you can also edit your video to add an end screen using your preferred video editing suite or software.

Now that you have set up your channel for success and are creating great content (and uploading it regularly) so that you can drive up your rapidly growing audience, you should start to consider monetizing your channel, which we shall talk about in within the chapters of the next section.

For the moment though, it is important to mention that how potent an income strategy YouTube turns out to be for you will greatly rely on your ability to provide value in a niche market. How you do this, which will greatly determine how you approach the endeavor, will depend on your niche and what you want your channel to accomplish in the end.

As long as you are providing value, your channel will grow and continue to grow to a point where your audiences consider you an authority and are willing to pay you to consume more of your content, and where sponsors approach you for collaboration on interesting projects that pay you well because they want access to your audience.

You can start monetizing your content from the first video (even before you create tons of content) or start monetizing after you have created several videos and a growing audience. The great thing is that as you learn more about YouTube marketing and creating a shareable and interactive YouTube channel, your ability to grow your channel in every way possible—including engagement, views, subscribers, and monetization—will also improve.

To learn more about growing your YouTube channel the right way, you can read the content on https://www.socialmediaexaminer.com/15-tips-growing-youtube-channel/ resource. While we have adeptly covered most of these YouTube growth hacks, Jeremy West, A YouTube certified, top, YouTube-for-business expert whose channel and various videos have attracted over a billion views, has some gems and a great perspective on the topic

YouTube should only be one part of your monetization strategy. YouTube is usually at the top end of a marketing funnel—since YouTube is a tool used to gain the attention of potential audiences.

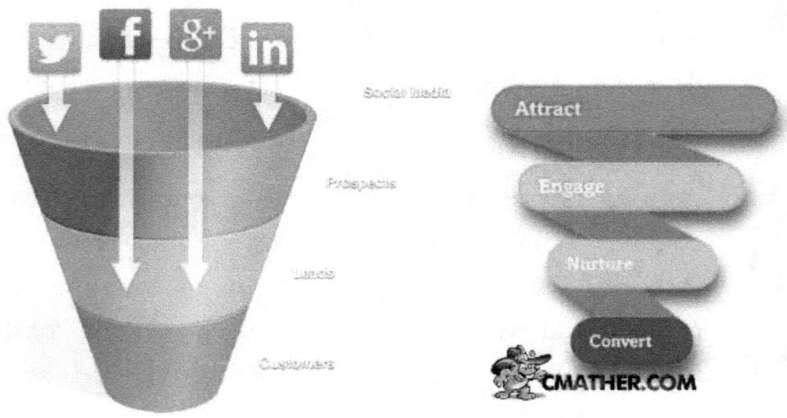

To monetize your channel, drive your YouTube followers to specific pages on your website (or even YouTube videos) where you can then ask them to take an action. The action can be to an offer intended to capture their email, or a sale pitch to promote a product you feel would help them achieve their desired end—which can be a landing page or video that sells something the audience wants.

This is the simplest trick to monetizing a YouTube channel the right and simple way. Remember that your ability to monetize your channel will largely depend on your niche, the value you create within it, and how you go about ensuring that your target audience sees this value and interacts with it.

Once you can do this, you can monetize using various avenues as discussed in the next section.

SECTION 3: YOUTUBE MONETIZATION - HOW TO IMPLEMENT THE MOST EFFECTIVE YOUTUBE MONETIZATION STRATEGIES

How you monetize your channel—including how long it takes your channel to start running itself and paying you (in terms of revenue generated)—will depend on your approach.

If you approach YouTube marketing as you would a business—one driven by your passions notwithstanding—you will put time and effort to creating a great YouTube channel that uploads great content consistently and whose content users consider valuable in whichever sense. Because of this, your audience will grow fast (and continue growing) so that in the end, you can monetize fast and grow your revenues even faster.

If, on the other hand, you approach it as a hobby, your effort to monetize your YouTube channel or grow your views, shares, and subscribes, will take longer since you will not be actively interacting with your intended targets regularly.

If you learn nothing else from this section, let what you learn to be that *"To create a great YouTube channel that generates revenue, you have to provide immense value consistently and in whichever format or way most appealing to your target audiences."*

If you do this, your channel will grow fast and start generating revenue even faster; how much revenue will depend on individual niches as well as how you monetize your YouTube channel since there are many ways to do so.

YOUTUBE MONETIZATION STRATEGIES: HOW TO MONETIZE YOUR YOUTUBE CHANNEL FOR RECURRING PASSIVE INCOME

We have various ways through which you can turn your amazing YouTube channel into a revenue-generating machine. This chapter discusses the most effective of these strategies and outlines how you can infuse them into your marketing strategy.

YouTube Partner Program (YPP): The Easiest Way to Monetize a Successful YouTube Channel

Since you have a keen interest in creating a successful YouTube channel that pays you and for its upkeep, you know that the easiest way to monetize your YouTube content is to serve ads on your content. This simply means allowing Google to serve your audience, relevant, audience-based ads, ads paid for by advertisers—revenue that Google shares with you, which is how you generate revenue.

The online space has tons of content on how to add Google adverts to your content. You can read more https://support.google.com/youtube/troubleshooter/7367438?hl=en#ts=7367346.

After having a difficult year in 2017—difficulty in terms of advertisers' backlash because of the metrics Google uses to serve specific videos on specific channels—Google has chosen to change their metrics to ensure that the adverts served on videos and channels are in line with brand marketing and that ads run on relevant content. They now have a stricter policy for those looking to monetize using ads

115

Previously, to monetize your channel, you needed a minimum of 10,000 cumulative views (on all your videos) to gain eligibility to the partner program (YPP):

Google has been using this to determine which channels can run adds. Since Google considers letting you run ads a privilege, they have stopped basing their acceptance into the partner program on mere views.

Today, they take into account audience engagement, channel size, the frequency of upload, social shares, and various other factors to determine which channels they give the right to run ads. Google now only gives the ability to run ads to channels that have a subscriber list larger than 1,000 and 4,000 hours of content uploaded within the last 12 months.

Size is not the only metric they use. In their bid to determine a channel's compatibility with their partner program, they also use other signals such as spam, likes, community strikes, and abuse flags.

Their need to implement these "hard-to-game user signals" is in line with their purpose: to serve users the most relevant, high-quality content and at the same time reward YouTube creators (that means you) who are helping them provide their users with engaging content that helps them fulfill their needs.

Google is also changing their metrics for Google Preferred with the intent being to ensure that the platform serves the most popular and highly valuable content on YouTube using vetting measurements such as engagement, views, channel subscribers, and other metrics such a social shares and SEOP optimization.

With that said, as long as you are providing immense value to your constantly growing audience, YouTube Partner Program is the simplest way to monetize your YouTube channels since, as long as your channel meets their guidelines and thresholds, Google will give you access to the program and you can start using it to monetize your channel.

The great thing about the platform is that it allows you great flexibility in determining where the ads appear.

YPP Ads for monetization: key takeaways and the money potential

How much you stand to earn from running ads on your YouTube video depends largely on your daily video views and engagement.

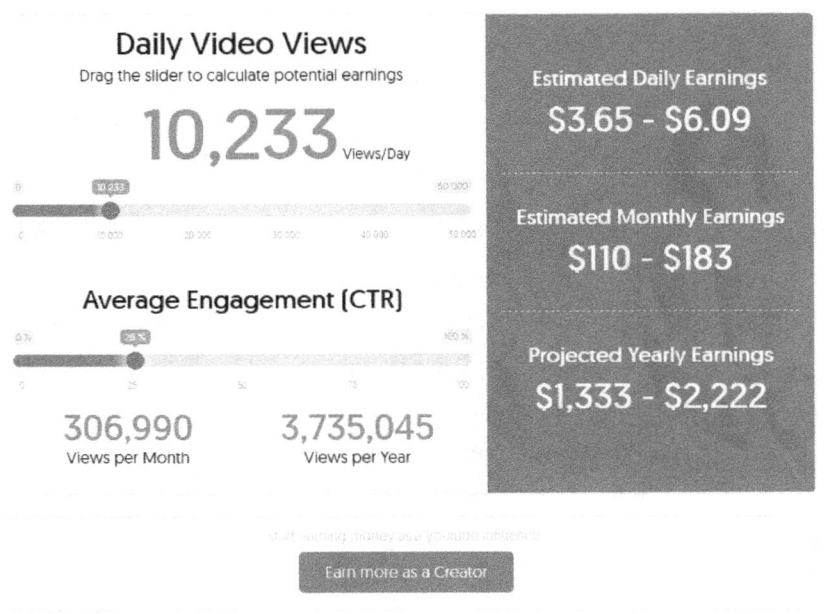

You can use the calculator https://influencermarketinghub.com/youtube-money-calculator/

to determine your potential earnings. With that in mind, however, remember that your daily views and engagement will determine four other factors that are central to how much you actually end up earning through YouTube partnership program.

The *"cost per click"* (CPC), how much Google pays you for users who click on the ad or watch an ad, will determine your conversion rate. Your *"estimated gross income for every 1,000 views,"* which is how much Google pays out for an average 1,000 ad views for channels within your niche. Your *"estimated earnings per subscriber"* will also factor in, and so will your *"estimated variance based on video engagement."*

Growing you channel expeditiously is the best way to earn more income because the more people you have viewing your content and engaging with it—commenting, sharing, etc.—the higher the number of people seeing and clicking the ads Google serves on your channel and videos, and the higher your revenue earning potential.

Uniting your successful YouTube channel for the Google partner program is the best and easiest way to monetize your YouTube channel. With that said, how much income you actually generate from servings ads this way will be dismal ($100 or less per month), which may not be enough to sustain your channel and your ability to create better valuable content. Hence, you should constantly work to diversify your earnings using other avenues.

These avenues include:

Diversify Your Earnings: Sponsorship For More YouTube Revenue

Sponsorships are a great way to generate revenue from YouTube once your views, engagement, and subscriber list is at a healthy level.

To use sponsorship, you can collaborate with other brands, channels, and great businesses within your niche, and then use mentions and video plugs to drive traffic and sales to specific product pages and using affiliate marketing, earn a commission of the sale price every time one of your valued followers uses your link to buy something you have recommended.

Still in relation to sponsorship, once you have a healthy following, build a community around your niche topic, and establish your authority and trust-ability within your niche, you can approach businesses you would like to partner with (or promote their product), and for a fee, allow them access to your audience.

Video logs (Vlogs) especially those in a series/playlist-like manner, are especially effective ways to generate YouTube passive income from sponsorships. You can infuse all forms of sponsorship (even affiliate marketing) into your video content through product reveals and show-offs. This approach is especially effective in the fashion niche (or any niche primary concentrated in products) where you buy products and reveal them as you talk about the products or demonstrate how they are helping make your life better (showing off products). In both cases, you tell viewers the value the product adds to your life and to theirs if they buy, so that when you seamlessly place a sponsored link to the product on your video content (Your YouTube video description area is a great place to do this), users can click and head over to buy the product. When they buy the product, you earn money from the sponsor.

You can also earn money from sponsorship by including product mention in the pre-roll, mid-roll, and end-roll segments of your YouTube content; these types of sponsorships are especially common and effective because they capitalize on visuals.

You can also generate tons of income from creating products reviews. Here, you can choose to create how to use video tutorials on products you use or of interest to your target audience and then integrate links to the product page (or ask the company to sponsor the video). By integrating links within the product video and the video description, you can easily compel your audience to take action that earns you commissions in revenue.

There are tons of ways to leverage your growing YouTube channel to generate revenue. For instance, once your channel shows sustainable growth over time or blows up and goes viral thus helping you create a sustainable business brand, you can choose to sell branded merchandise such as T-shirts, mugs, canvas bags, or any other forms of merchandise on Amazon Merch or using the various online shopping channels.

Moreover, once you have a ready audience, you can also monetize your YouTube viewership by creating digital products such as eBooks, video course or tutorials. As long as you are providing value and users are appreciating this value—which therefore means your channel is growing and you are consistently creating new content—you will never lack ways to monetize your YouTube viewership.

Creating value is more important than monetization because in the end, how much value you create will determine your status within your niche, which shall in effect determine how much your YouTube channel earns.

Before you monetize, therefore, concentrate on providing immense value by providing video content that woos and wows your targeted audience. If you do this really well, the money will surely follow and surpass your expectations. In fact, creating a valuable YouTube channel is how you become a YouTube influencer who generates millions in passive income from YouTube.

Contrary to popular belief, monetizing your YouTube channel is actually the easiest part of the process. Once you provide an audience immense value, they will be more than willing to pay you well for it (this is where you can create your own digital products, collaborate with other brands and business to promote their products and earn affiliate commissions, or even allow advertisers access to your audience through sponsored listings).

Obviously, creating value is but the first step in the process. After producing your valuable video content, you have to edit it to make it of high quality, and then after doing this, upload the video while optimizing it for search so that you can increase your views, subscriptions, shares, and thereby grow your channel.

To learn more about editing your YouTube video, read https://www.entrepreneur.com/article/226771 page.

Moreover, since the niche you pursue will determine how aggressively you can grow your channel—more niche popularity means more demand for valuable niche content—to grow your revenue (and inadvertently, your YouTube channel), encourage your audience to interact with your content. Ask them to comment and share the content they find most helpful on social media and to subscribe to your channel.

You can also grow your audience by adding a blog element to your YouTube business, which we talked about earlier by saying how an effective SEO strategy it is; that is how you create a successful YouTube channel that attracts millions of views and subscribers as well as one that rewards you well by generating an income.

CONCLUSION

If you implement the strategies discussed within this actionable YouTube success manual, there is no doubt in my mind that you will create a great and successful channel that pays you well.

Like most things, remember that growing a YouTube channel is a time and resource intensive endeavor. Pace yourself, and if you are relatively new to the prospect, give yourself ample time for growth. Remember that as you get started and go about implementing the numerous lessons outlined in each section, your skills as a YouTube creator will improve impressively, and the easier it will be to make your channel valuable and a capable cash-generating business.

We have come to the end of the book. Thank you for reading and congratulations on reading until the end.

If you found the book valuable, can you recommend it to others? One way to do that is to post a review on Amazon.

Thank you and good luck!

Get Your Free Copy of

How to be a Real Estate Millionaire

To Get Your Free Copy, Open the Link

https://ebraveboy_3ee2.gr8.com/

www.ingramcontent.com/pod-product-compliance
Lightning Source LLC
Chambersburg PA
CBHW072047230526
45468CB00019B/458